# A Research Guide
# for Undergraduate
# Students

FIFTH EDITION

# A Research Guide for Undergraduate Students

*English and American Literature*

NANCY L. BAKER

AND

NANCY HULING

The Modern Language Association of America
New York   2000

For information about obtaining permission to reprint material from MLA book publications, send your request by mail (see address below), e-mail (permissions@mla.org), or fax (646 458-0030).

Library of Congress Cataloging-in-Publication Data

Baker, Nancy L., 1950–
    A research guide for undergraduate students : English and American literature / Nancy L. Baker and Nancy Huling — 5th ed.
      p. cm.
    Includes bibliographical references and index.
    ISBN 0-87352-978-2 (pbk.)
      1. English literature—Research—Methodology. 2. American literature—Research—Methodology. 3. American literature—Bibliography. 4. English literature—Bibliography. I. Huling, Nancy, 1950– II. Title.

PR56 .B34 2000
820'.7'2—dc21                                  00-059291

The following publishers and authors have granted permission to reproduce materials from copyrighted works: Joseph Wiesenfarth for *Dictionary of Literary Biography*, vol. 21, *Victorian Novelists before 1885*; copyright 1983 by Gale Research Inc; reprinted by permission of the author. Innovative Interfaces Inc., Washington State University, and Eastern Washington University for *Griffin*, the online public access catalog shared by Washington State University and Eastern Washington University; Innovative Interfaces Inc. and the University of Washington for the UW Libraries Catalog. Georg Olms Verlag for Martin Spevack, *The Harvard Concordance to Shakespeare*; copyright 1973 by Georg Olms Verlag. Oxford University Press for *The Oxford English Dictionary*, second edition; copyright 1989 by Oxford University Press; reprinted by permission of Oxford University Press. Oxford University Press for *The Oxford Companion to Women's Writing in the United States*, edited by Cathy N. Davidson et al.; copyright 1995 by Oxford University Press; used by permission of Oxford University Press, Inc. University of Toronto Press for *Wellesley Index to Victorian Periodicals*, vol. 1, entries 509–11; copyright 1966 by University of Toronto Press. The University of Oklahoma for *World Literature Today*; copyright 1996 by the University of Oklahoma. H. W. Wilson Company for *Book Review Digest*; copyright 1996 by H. W. Wilson Company; materials reproduced by permission of the publisher. H. W. Wilson Company for *Humanities Index*; copyright 1999 by the H. W. Wilson Company; materials reproduced by permission of the publisher. OCLC Online Computer Library Center, Inc., for the *FirstSearch* database; *FirstSearch* is a registered trademark of OCLC Online Computer Library Center, Inc. SilverPlatter Information, Inc., for software and database structure of the *MLA International Bibliography* database; copyright 1990–2000 by SilverPlatter Information, Inc.; Modern Language Association of America for information copyright of the *MLA International Bibliography*; copyright 1963–2000 by The Modern Language Association of America; all rights reserved. Bell & Howell Information and Learning Company for *ProQuest*; further reproduction is prohibited without permission. Chadwyck-Healey, Inc., for *Literature Online*; copyright 1996–99 by Chadwyck-Healey, Ltd., and Chadwyck-Healey, Inc. The Regents of the University of California for *Melvyl* Catalog database; copyright 1999 by The Regents of the University of California; *Melvyl* is a registered trademark of the Regents of the University of California. The Gale Group for *Expanded Academic ASAP*; copyright 2000 by The Gale Group. The Gale Group for *Book Review Index*; copyright 1996 by The Gale Group. University of Washington, Department of English, for *Selected Links to Other Websites*.

Published by The Modern Language Association of America
26 Broadway, New York, New York 10004-1789
www.mla.org

# Contents

# Preface to the Fifth Edition

In 1982, when the first edition of this literary research guide was published, the microcomputer revolution was a phenomenon waiting to happen. The first edition was written on an electric typewriter. Just three years later, when the second edition was drafted, this typewriter was retired to the attic and replaced by a Kaypro personal computer with a CP/M operating system. By 1989, the Kaypro had joined the electric typewriter in the attic, and a more sophisticated Macintosh SE/30 was used to write the third edition. We wrote the fourth edition on a more powerful Macintosh, a Quadra 610. The fifth edition was typed on an IBM Thinkpad 385ED, which was also used to consult many of the electronic reference sources discussed in our guide. This personal technological history in no way represents state-of-the-art developments in the greater world of automation. Nevertheless, it is symbolic, in its modest way, of an even more dramatic electronic metamorphosis undertaken by libraries during this same period.

The microcomputer, which has reshaped so many aspects of our lives, has transformed even that most humanistic pursuit, literary research. Whereas the first edition of our guide spoke of card catalogs and printed indexes, electronic catalogs and indexes are now the norm. Although printed versions of many reference books are still available and will always be in our libraries, it is virtually impossible to get students to use them if an automated alternative is available. We consulted many of the sources discussed in this guide from a distance, in our offices or homes, over an electronic network. This method of retrieving information will increasingly become the norm.

The bewildering pace of these changes will continue to escalate.

Some have speculated that by the beginning of the twenty-first century ninety-eight percent of all new information will be created and stored in digital format. From the time this book goes to press to the time it reaches you, many new automated resources will become available in your libraries and over the Internet, and those we have mentioned will have been enhanced. Although this guide will not have discussed all these resources and enhancements, it should give you a solid foundation on which to master them as they become available.

For this edition of *A Research Guide for Undergraduate Students: English and American Literature*, we would like to acknowledge Helene Williams, English studies librarian at the University of Washington, for her willingness to discuss current undergraduate literary research needs, for recommending real-life topics to use as examples, and for providing insights on the uses of primary sources as they relate to literary study. Special thanks to Cynthia Stewart Kaag, head of the Frances Penrose Owen Science and Engineering Library at Washington State University, for her insights on *EndNote* and *ProCite*. Without the help of our colleagues in the reference departments of the Suzzallo and Allen Libraries at the University of Washington and the Holland/New Library at Washington State University, this book would not have been possible. Charles A. Carpenter, now retired professor of English at the State University of New York, Binghamton, planted the seed that brought forth the original version of this guide. Special thanks to our spouses, James Baker and Richard Huling, and to the Huling children, without whose encouragement and support this edition would never have been completed. Special thanks, as well, to Lorena O'English for indexing this guide. Last but hardly least, our sincerest thanks to the readers and editors at the Modern Language Association.

As the publication of a fifth edition implies, we have been gratified by the success of this modest guide for undergraduate students. We hope this little book continues to prove profitable to its readers.

Nancy L. Baker
*University of Iowa*

Nancy Huling
*University of Washington*

# Introduction:
# The Research Process

This brief guide to research methods in English and American literature is written for you, the undergraduate student. Most other research guides to literature are written for graduate students and advanced scholars, who have more experience with the library and who may need exhaustive lists of numerous specialized reference works. None of the other guides effectively deals with your problems as a library user.

Over twenty-five years of academic library experience has convinced us that your research requirements are special. Because your time and the scope of your work are both limited, you are unlikely to need many of the specialized reference sources accessible through the library. But most undergraduate students are not familiar enough with the basic tools and the organization of the library to use their research time efficiently. They often find the research process frustrating. When they cannot find what they need, they often assume it is simply not available. Almost always they're wrong; they simply do not know how to locate what they want.

Keeping this in mind, you should not be surprised that this guide concentrates on the search for secondary sources, those materials that analyze and criticize an author's work. As an undergraduate you rarely deal with problems involving primary sources—for example, the various editions of an author's works. But since it has grown increasingly common for undergraduates to consult primary sources, particularly for multidisciplinary research, we have provided some guidance on the use of these kinds of sources. This guide stresses the fifty or so literary research tools that are most likely to be useful to you. An annotated list of about seventy is appended for further study.

This guide also discusses basic research strategy. It presents a systematic way of locating important books and articles on English and American literature. Such a search strategy involves more than just a quick perusal of your library's online public access catalog or the first electronic index you might find. To be thorough, you should seek all pertinent articles and books on your subject. Then, even if many of these articles and books prove irrelevant to your topic, you can be confident that you have not overlooked any major studies. Moreover, by structuring your research systematically, you can spend most of your time in writing your term paper rather than in searching for materials.

The research process is a fluid one. No single strategy is entirely successful for every problem. In suggesting a systematic approach to research, we do not mean to reduce a creative and interpretative process to a rigid lockstep. For some research problems, certain chapters of this guide do not apply at all. For many topics, the strategy and sources discussed in the first four chapters may provide all the assistance you need. In addition, you will find the research process is often cyclical, and it may be necessary to repeat some steps depending on your findings at a later step. Individual problems require their own research strategies.

From this guide you should gain a basic understanding of what various types of reference sources can and cannot do; a working familiarity with the major indexes, bibliographies, and other research tools in literature; some tips on consulting electronic resources effectively; a taste of how to work with primary sources; and an idea of systematic research methods. The quality of your term papers should improve along with the efficiency and productivity of your research efforts.

# CHAPTER ONE

# Conducting Research in an Electronic Environment

The world of information has undergone rapid changes in the last five years, significantly affecting how knowledge is stored and transmitted. Literary research has felt these changes. Libraries increasingly subscribe to electronic databases that provide complete texts of periodical and newspaper articles on the World Wide Web. Through such endeavors as *Project Muse* and *JSTOR*, many scholarly journals have been digitized and made available to libraries on the Web through subscription. And thousands of Web sites exist on an array of topics.

Doubtless you have used computers for much of your life—finding information for your classes, listening to music, performing calculations, writing papers. Despite the growth in the number of electronic sources, including literary texts, research in literature continues to rely heavily on print resources. This mixed environment of print and electronic sources creates challenges for the researcher. Although you may locate an article from a periodical or even an entire novel online, book-length critical studies continue to be published in paper format.

It is clearly tempting, as you sit in your residence hall or apartment, to rely only on those articles that you can find in full text through your computer. There may be times when this is appropriate, particularly for short, concentrated assignments. But many research projects will require a careful evaluation of the references you retrieve through your searches, and the best articles for your particular topic may be available only in print format in your library. It is important to consider quality when you opt for the rapid availability of a full-text online source over a source available only through a trip to the library.

Beyond the growing ability to find scholarly articles online, there seems to be a widespread belief that almost everything worth reading now is available for free on the Web. Indeed, a search of the Web for Jane Austen turns up almost 20,000 matches, a figure that increases daily. Most of the references are pieces of a Jane Austen information page, but a short paper called "Class Distinctions in Jane Austen's Era" also turns up. The title sounds like a solid piece of research, but there is no clear indication of author or origin, nor are any sources of information cited. Using the information found in this paper would be a mistake, given its uncertain authority. Anyone can create an easily accessible Web site. Compare this with the scholarly publishing process. Before an article is published in an academic (or refereed) periodical, it is reviewed by two or three other scholars in the field who comment on the thesis, suggest changes, or even reject it for publication. Consequently, periodical articles found through searching the electronic databases discussed later in this book have gone through a rigorous review process before publication. These databases, whether on the Web or on CD-ROM, are not free; your library pays for access for students and faculty members at your college or university.

What kind of literary information can you expect to find when conducting a general search of the Web using a search engine, such as *Google* or *Alta Vista*? Fans of various authors have created Web sites, some of them quite large, on which they post a wide array of material, mostly nonscholarly. Going back to our search of Jane Austen, we also find outlines for college courses, bibliographies of criticism posted by librarians, guides to library collections of her works, and the page for the Jane Austen Society of North America. Digging through all these sites for criticism on Austen would not be an effective use of time, given the large body of criticism easily found by searching some of the standard databases mentioned later in this book. But a general Web search for a contemporary author may be worthwhile. For example, a search for information on Sherman Alexie finds the "official sherman alexie site," from *fallsapart productions* (http://www.fallsapart.com/). This site includes a biography, a bibliography of Alexie's works with links to tables of contents, a listing of articles about Alexie (some with text), upcoming projects, book discussions, and more. If you decide to explore the Web extensively for literary sites, it is a good idea to consult the "help" screens of the search engines you use to learn about the advanced features. Many of the search engines, although not as sophisticated as electronic databases offered through libraries, do permit the use of connector words such as *and* and *or*. It is important to note that no single search engine scans and returns results from the entire Web.

Web search engines are generally not the most effective method for finding quality sites related to literature. A recent search found over 1,700 sites mentioning Sherman Alexie. Even when the search engine returns the results ranked by relevance, you will still need to examine a considerable amount of information. A better strategy for finding Web sites related to the study of literature is to check the Web sites of your library and your English department. The librarian responsible for developing the collection in English and American literature has likely put together a Web page that provides links to well-organized and authoritative sites. English departments have similar lists, and individual faculty members often create sites focusing on their specialties, such as the Victorian period, medieval literature, and so forth. For example, the University of Washington's English department provides as part of its Web page the link "Literature and Humanities Resources on the Web" (fig. 1). Two of the sources, "Literary Resources on the Net" (http://andromeda.rutgers.edu/~jlynch/Lit/) and "Voice of the Shuttle" (http://vos.ucsb.edu/) are highly recommended in James Harner's *Literary Research Guide* as "sites that offer a judicious selection of current guides to specific Internet resources" (see app., sec. 1). These sites were created and are maintained by faculty members. Remember that Web site addresses may change, so saving these sites through the "bookmarks" or "favorites" function on your computer will help you stay current.

Your evaluation of sources uncovered during a "free" search of the Web is critical. Ask yourself questions: Who is the author? What is the context? Has the site been updated recently? Can the information be verified elsewhere? What is the value of the information found on the

# University of Washington
# Department of English

## Selected Links to Other Websites

Most of the following links contain collections of links to a variety of related sites and web pages:

Literature and Humanities Resources on the Web
Colleges and Universities on the Web
English Departments on the Web
Electronic Texts on the Web
A Few Authors and Topics

## Literature and Humanities Resources on the Web

The English Server
Resources for humanities research, texts in arts and humanities, and more.

HUMBUL
HUManities BULletin board. Extensive humanities links.

A Literary Index
Internet Resources in Literature

Literary Resources on the Net
Links to literature and humanities sites.

Voice of the Shuttle
Extensive humanities research resources.

Fig. 1. University of Washington, Department of English, *Selected Links to Other Websites.*

Web site compared with the range of information on the topic? How does the site compare with other sources? (Actually, these same questions can help you evaluate all the information sources, electronic and printed, discussed throughout this book.) You will want to make sure that what you use and cite in support of your research is valid and appropriate for your level of work and not merely a paper posted to the Web by a third grader who may have obtained much of his or her information from an encyclopedia (this situation has actually happened!). In the appendix, you find references to sources that will help you evaluate Web sites.

Despite the pitfalls highlighted here, electronic databases and the World Wide Web have been a boon to student research. As universities and colleges provide remote access to full-text article databases, students can do a substantial amount of research outside the library, independent of building hours. Waiting until the last minute to research and write your paper is still not a wise idea, however, since the best source that you find on your computer at 2:00 a.m. may still be a print periodical or book available only in the library. Your most important goal is to locate and use the best possible sources for your research, whether they are paper or electronic.

# CHAPTER TWO

# Searching for Books

## Checking Your Library's Catalog

One of the first resources you will need to master for literary research is your library's catalog of the books, periodicals, and other collections on its shelves or available electronically. For quite some time, card catalogs served this purpose. Your library has undoubtedly replaced its card catalog with microcomputers offering an electronic listing of your library's holdings. These electronic catalogs are typically called online public access catalogs or online catalogs. If your library is still adding entries for older materials into your online catalog, it must keep the card catalog available until all these titles have been entered into the online catalog's database. If so, you may need to consult both catalogs to make sure that you have not overlooked pertinent materials. Since online catalogs evolved from their printed predecessors, the two formats have much in common. However, most online catalogs offer many more ways to search for pertinent material than card catalogs can. In addition, you can probably consult your online catalog remotely from home if you have a microcomputer and modem.

Not all online catalogs look the same or have the same features. There are probably a dozen or so companies offering online catalog software suitable for college and university libraries. Two libraries with online catalogs from the same company may have chosen different options and features. Some universities have designed and created their own unique online catalogs. Since it would be impossible to describe the features of all online catalogs, we have chosen a typical one shared by Washington State University (WSU) and Eastern Washington University (EWU). This online catalog is called *Griffin* for the mythical beast whose body combines a cougar and an eagle, the respective mascots for these two universities. Libraries frequently assign a catchy acronym or name like *Griffin* to their online catalogs. The software for *Griffin* was developed by a company called Innovative Interfaces Inc.

When you call up the first screen in *Griffin*, you will notice that this is a Web-based catalog. Those of you who surf the Internet will feel right at home with this catalog. If you do not have a Web browser

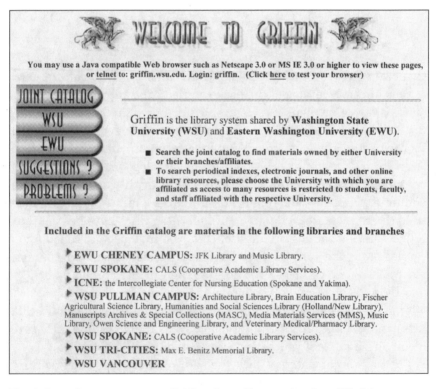

Fig. 2. Introductory screen to *Griffin*, the online catalog from Washington State University and Eastern Washington University.

like Netscape, you can still access a text-based version of the catalog by using Telnet. For the purposes of this chapter, we will be using the Web version that you would use if you consulted *Griffin* from the microcomputers available in the libraries at WSU or EWU.

From the initial welcome screen, you will notice that WSU and EWU are decentralized campuses; that is, there are libraries located on their various branch campuses around the state. In addition, Washington State University has six libraries on its main Pullman campus. The "joint catalog" includes the holdings of all these libraries. For convenience, it is possible to consult just the library at the user's branch campus. A WSU student on the main campus in Pullman might prefer to see only those books that are available at any of the WSU campuses rather than those that are owned by EWU. For purposes of illustration, we will consult the joint catalog.

Using your mouse, click on the bar in the upper left corner labeled "joint catalog" (fig. 2). You can always tell which part of the joint catalog you are searching by looking at the pull-down bar near the top of the main search screen. There are eleven different ways to search *Griffin*: by author, title, author and title, keyword, subject headings, and six different kinds of numbers including Library of Congress and Dewey decimal call numbers (fig. 3).

Let's assume you want to search for books written by Albert von Frank. To complete an author search, simply click on the bar labeled "author" and then type "von frank, albert" in the space provided (fig. 4). Six items match your request (fig. 5). If you are interested in item 3, *The Sacred Game: Provincialism and Frontier Consciousness in American Literature, 1630–1860,* click on the title (highlighted in blue) and you will be given a more complete bibliographic record, including place of publication, publisher, and date of publication (fig. 6). From the location key, you learn that there are two copies of this book at WSU in the Holland Library. Adjacent to the call numbers is the circulation status for each. One of the copies is currently checked out to a borrower and due 8-23-00; the second copy is "on shelf" and available to be checked out. A book may be missing or its availability restricted. The remainder of the entry lists additional bibliographic information for this title, including five Library of Congress subject headings that reflect the subject of

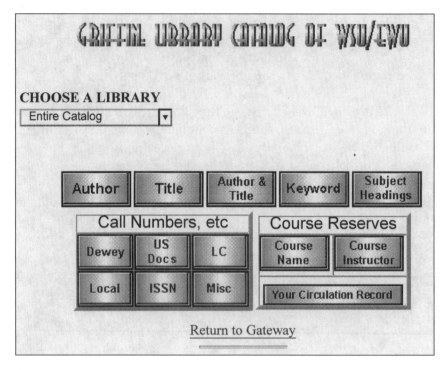

Fig. 3. Search options screen on *Griffin*.

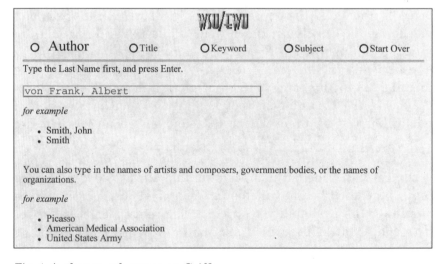

Fig. 4. Author search screen on *Griffin*.

| Num | Mark | AUTHORS (1-6 of 6) | Year | Entries |
|---|---|---|---|---|
| **Von Frank Albert J** | | | | |
| 1 | ☐ | Critical Essays On Hawthorne's Short Stories / Albert J. Von Frank. | 1991 | 1 |
| 2 | ☐ | An Emerson Chronology / Albert J. Von Frank. | 1994 | 1 |
| 3 | ☐ | The Sacred Game : Provincialism And Frontier Consciousness In American Literature, 1630-1860 / Albert J. Von Frank. | 1985 | 1 |
| 4 | ☐ | Sermons | 1989-c1992. | 1 |
| 5 | ☐ | The Trials Of Anthony Burns : Freedom And Slavery In Emerson's Boston / Albert J. Von Frank. | 1998 | 1 |
| 6 | ☐ | Whittier : A Comprehensive Annotated Bibliography / By Albert J. Von Frank. | 1976 | 1 |

Save Marked Records

Extended Display    Start Over    Another Search    Limit/Sort

Fig. 5. The listing of books by Albert J. Von Frank in *Griffin*.

Record 3 of 6

| | |
|---|---|
| *Author* | Von Frank, Albert J. |
| *Title* | **The sacred game : provincialism and frontier consciousness in American literature, 1630-1860 / Albert J. von Frank.** |
| *Imprint* | Cambridge [Cambridgeshire] ; New York : Cambridge University Press, 1985. |

| LOCATION | CALL NUMBER | STATUS |
|---|---|---|
| WSU Holland | PS169.F7 V66 1985 | DUE 08-23-00 |
| WSU Holland | PS169.F7 V66 1985 c.2 | ON SHELF |

| | |
|---|---|
| *Description* | viii, 188 p. ; 24 cm. |
| *Series* | Cambridge studies in American literature and culture |
| | Cambridge studies in American literature and culture. |
| *Bibliog.* | Bibliography: p. 159-183. |
| *Note* | Includes index. |
| *Subject* | American literature -- History and criticism. |
| | Frontier and pioneer life in literature. |
| | Regionalism in literature. |
| | National characteristics, American, in literature. |
| | United States -- Civilization. |
| *ISBN* | 0521301599 |
| *Misc no* | WSU000403077 |

Previous Record    Next Record    Return to Browse    Another Search    Start Over    Marc Display

Export

Fig. 6. The listing for Albert J. Von Frank's *The Sacred Game* in *Griffin*.

the book. These subject headings could come in handy if you want to locate other books on the same subject.

The six bars at the bottom of the screen allow you to move around the database quickly. You can check the previous record—in this case, item 2 on the list of von Frank titles—or you can move to the next record, item 4 in the list. The "return to browse" key will take you back to the list of six items that matched "von frank, albert," or you can begin another author search by clicking on "another search." If you want to begin a search other than by author, click on "start over" and the system will take you back to the screen in figure 1. A MARC display is a very detailed cataloging record that is most useful to librarians. Finally, if you want to send this record to your e-mail, you can "export" it. This is especially helpful if you are sorting through a lot of catalog records and want to compile a convenient list of the most useful titles. This is easily accomplished by clicking on the boxes to the left of the entries that are more promising. You can then forward this list to yourself by e-mail.

To conduct a title search, click on the title bar in figure 3, and then type the title in the space provided. For example, if you are seeking a copy of *Comic Women, Tragic Men: A Study of Gender and Genre in*

| Author | Bamber, Linda. |
|--------|----------------|
| Title | **Comic women, tragic men : a study of gender and genre in Shakespeare / Linda Bamber.** |
| Imprint | Stanford, Calif. : Stanford University Press, 1982. |

| LOCATION | CALL NUMBER | STATUS |
|----------|-------------|--------|
| EWU JFK Stacks | PR2989 .B3 1982 | ON SHELF |
| WSU Holland | PR2989 .B3 1982 | ON SHELF |

| Description | 211 p. ; 23 cm. |
|-------------|-----------------|
| Bibliog. | Includes bibliographical references and index. |
| Subject | Shakespeare, William, 1564-1616 -- Characters. |
| | Sex role in literature. |
| | Self in literature. |
| | Literary form. |
| ISBN | 0804711267 |
| Misc no | WSU000281015 |
| | (OCoLC)08624055 |

| Previous Record | Next Record | Another Search | Start Over | Marc Display | Export |
|-----------------|-------------|----------------|------------|--------------|--------|

Fig. 7. The listing for Linda Bamber's *Comic Women, Tragic Men* in *Griffin*.

*Shakespeare,* by Linda Bamber, simply type "comic women, tragic men." Two copies of the book are available, one at WSU and one at EWU (fig. 7).

The author and title search is especially useful when you are searching prolific authors or common titles, (e.g., *Works*). In such cases, a search by author or by title is apt to produce a long list of citations that do not meet your needs. Combining both author and title will narrow the resulting matches considerably.

Although author, title, or author and title searches are generally straightforward, it is always advisable to try a different approach if one of them proves unsuccessful. You may have the title slightly incorrect or may have the author's name misspelled.

A thorough subject search can be more roundabout. Many online catalogs allow you to search keywords in the title. Provided the author has titled his or her book with substantive keywords, this kind of search can be fruitful. You should be aware, however, that when a book is cataloged, subject headings approved by the Library of Congress are assigned to that book. In a traditional card catalog, these formal subject headings provide the only subject access.

*Griffin* offers both keyword searching—using the connectors "and," "not," and "or"—and access by Library of Congress subject headings. In this online catalog, the keyword searches are matched against the title, subjects, and content notes in the bibliographic record. This can be a plus or a minus depending on the succinctness of your keywords. For example, if you want to find books on the depiction of prostitutes in Victorian literature and you type the keywords "prostitutes and Victorian and literature," three titles emerge that are right on target (fig. 8). All three titles—*Fallenness in Victorian Women's Writing: Marry, Stitch, Die, or Do Worse; Tainted Souls and Painted Faces: The Rhetoric of Fallenness in Victorian Culture*; and *Walking the Victorian Streets: Women, Representation, and the City*—were identified as pertinent only because the terms "prostitutes" and "literature" match terms from the subject headings. "Victorian" is the only term of the three to match any of these three titles (fig. 9). In this case, the ability to match keywords in the title, subjects, and content notes is clearly a plus. However, if you want to find books about how childhood is portrayed in the novels of Jane Austen and you use "Austen and

PROSTITUTES is in 102 titles.
VICTORIAN is in 1747 titles.
LITERATURE is in 63331 titles.
Both "PROSTITUTES" and "VICTORIAN" are in 5 titles.
Adding "LITERATURE" leaves 3 titles.
There are 3 entries with PROSTITUTES, VICTORIAN & LITERATURE.

| Num | Mark | WORDS (1-3 of 3) | Entries 3 Found |
|---|---|---|---|
| 1 | ☐ | Fallenness in Victorian women's writing : marry, stitch, die | 1 |
| 2 | ☐ | Tainted souls and painted faces : the rhetoric of fallenness | 1 |
| 3 | ☐ | Walking the Victorian streets : women, representation, and t | 1 |

Save Marked Records

Extended Display | Start Over | Another Search | Limit/Sort

Fig. 8. The entries matching keywords *prostitutes*, *Victorian*, and *literature* in *Griffin*.

| *Author* | Logan, Deborah Anna, 1951- |
|---|---|
| *Title* | **Fallenness in Victorian women's writing : marry, stitch, die, or do worse / Deborah Anna Logan.** |
| *Imprint* | Columbia : University of Missouri Press, c1998. |

| LOCATION | CALL NUMBER | STATUS |
|---|---|---|
| WSU Holland | PR115 .L64 1998 | ON SHELF |
| EWU JFK Stacks | PR115 .L64 1998 | ON SHELF |

| *Description* | x, 236 p. ; 24 cm. |
|---|---|
| *Bibliog.* | Includes bibliographical references and index. |
| *Subject* | English **literature** -- Women authors -- History and criticism. |
| | Women and **literature** -- Great Britain -- History -- 19th century. |
| | English **literature** -- 19th century -- History and criticism. |
| | Unmarried mothers in **literature**. |
| | Moral conditions in **literature**. |
| | Social problems in **literature**. |
| | Prostitution in **literature**. |
| | **Prostitutes** in **literature**. |
| | Women in **literature**. |
| *ISBN* | 0826211755 (alk. paper) |

Next Record | Return to Browse | Another Search | Start Over | Marc Display | Export

Fig. 9. The listing for Deborah Logan's *Fallenness in Victorian Women's Writing* in *Griffin*.

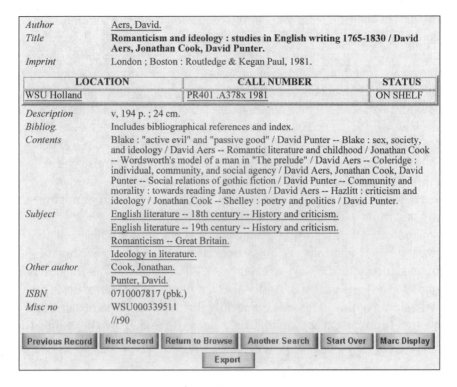

| Author | Aers, David. |
| --- | --- |
| Title | **Romanticism and ideology : studies in English writing 1765-1830 / David Aers, Jonathan Cook, David Punter.** |
| Imprint | London ; Boston : Routledge & Kegan Paul, 1981. |

| LOCATION | CALL NUMBER | STATUS |
| --- | --- | --- |
| WSU Holland | PR401 .A378x 1981 | ON SHELF |

| | |
| --- | --- |
| Description | v, 194 p. ; 24 cm. |
| Bibliog. | Includes bibliographical references and index. |
| Contents | Blake : "active evil" and "passive good" / David Punter -- Blake : sex, society, and ideology / David Aers -- Romantic literature and childhood / Jonathan Cook -- Wordsworth's model of a man in "The prelude" / David Aers -- Coleridge : individual, community, and social agency / David Aers, Jonathan Cook, David Punter -- Social relations of gothic fiction / David Punter -- Community and morality : towards reading Jane Austen / David Aers -- Hazlitt : criticism and ideology / Jonathan Cook -- Shelley : poetry and politics / David Punter. |
| Subject | English literature -- 18th century -- History and criticism. |
| | English literature -- 19th century -- History and criticism. |
| | Romanticism -- Great Britain. |
| | Ideology in literature. |
| Other author | Cook, Jonathan. |
| | Punter, David. |
| ISBN | 0710007817 (pbk.) |
| Misc no | WSU000339511 |
| | //r90 |

Previous Record | Next Record | Return to Browse | Another Search | Start Over | Marc Display

Export

Fig. 10. The listing for David Aers's *Romanticism and Ideology Writing* in *Griffin.*

childhood" in a keyword search, you will be disappointed by the result. *Griffin* matched the two terms from the content notes. Closer examination of these notes indicates that the essay about Austen has nothing to do with childhood and the one on childhood has nothing to do with Jane Austen (fig. 10). These false hits can occur when the database searches the entire record, including notes, for keywords.

Consider, for a moment, the reason for combining keywords together with connectors like "and." Assuming you seek books on madness in *Hamlet,* if you enter only "Hamlet" you will match over 550 entries in *Griffin*, including copies of the play in print, recordings of actual performances, and books of literary criticism that include "Hamlet" in the title, subject, or notes field. Some of these matches would be totally irrelevant titles with the English word *hamlet* (as in "a small village") in the title. Had you simply requested the term "madness" you would have retrieved an equally long list of books in psychiatry and psychology along with any other titles containing the word. By linking the terms together, you have narrowed your results to include only items that match both words. The result is a manageable list of nine titles, all pertinent to your topic. One of these titles, *Hamlet's Enemy: Madness and Myth in* Hamlet, is especially relevant (fig. 11). Had Theodore Lidz entitled his book *Hamlet's Enemy: Mental Illness and Myth in* Hamlet, your search would not have been successful, because you chose a different term for the idea of madness. Keyword searches always carry this risk. You need to think of the various synonyms the author might use and link them with "or," as in "madness or mental illness."

You can also avoid this problem if you search by Library of Congress subject headings. When a book is cataloged, subject headings are assigned to it. *Library of Congress Subject Headings* is the official guide to these headings. Usually shelved near the reference desk, this five-volume guide does not generally list personal names. Shakespeare, the one exception to this rule, is included in the guide to demonstrate the variety of subdivisions that can be used with an

| Author | Lidz, Theodore. |
|--------|-----------------|
| Title | **Hamlet's enemy : madness and myth in Hamlet / Theodore Lidz.** |
| Imprint | New York : Basic Books, [1975] |

| LOCATION | CALL NUMBER | STATUS |
|----------|-------------|--------|
| EWU JFK Stacks | PR2807 .L5 1975 | ON SHELF |
| WSU Holland | PR2807 .L5 1975 | ON SHELF |

| Description | xiii, 258 p. : ill. ; 24 cm. |
|-------------|------------------------------|
| Bibliog. | Bibliography: p. 243-246. |
| Note | Includes index. |
| Subject | Shakespeare, William, 1564-1616. **Hamlet**. |
| | Mental illness in literature. |
| | Shakespeare, William, 1564-1616. **Hamlet** -- Sources. |
| | Psychoanalysis and literature. |
| ISBN | 0465028179 |
| Misc no | WSU000220749 |
| | (OCoLC)01322185 |

| Previous Record | Next Record | Return to Browse | Another Search | Start Over | Marc Display |
|-----------------|-------------|------------------|----------------|------------|--------------|

| Export |
|--------|

Fig. 11. The listing for Theodore Lidz's *Hamlet's Enemy* in *Griffin*.

author's name as appropriate. Under the heading "Shakespeare, William, 1564–1616—Bibliography," you might find a critical bibliography that could be a good starting point for your research (fig. 12). Literary criticism on specific works will be listed under the author's name and dates and the name of the work. Criticism on *Hamlet,* for example, will be found under the heading "Shakespeare, William, 1564–1616. Hamlet." An important subdivision is "Criticism and interpretation," which is often used after the author's name to identify studies concerned with more than one of his or her works. You should familiarize yourself with these subdivisions. They may be used with other authors in English and American literature. Once you determine which subject heading is appropriate, simply click on the bar labeled "subject headings" (fig. 3) and type in the subject heading.

The online catalog itself can suggest appropriate subject headings. If you return to the entry by Albert von Frank (fig. 6), you will notice five subject headings assigned to that book. These subject headings

**Shakespeare, William, 1564-1616.   Hamlet**
- **— Bibliography**
- **— Concordances**
      BT  Shakespeare, William, 1564-1616—
          Concordances
- **— Congresses**
- **— Criticism, Textual**
      BT  Shakespeare, William, 1564-1616—
          Criticism, Textual
- **— Exhibitions**
- **— Illustrations**
      BT  Shakespeare, William, 1564-1616—
          Illustrations
- **— Indexes**
- **— Juvenile films**
- **— Juvenile literature**
- **— Juvenile sound recordings**
- **— Pictorial works**
- **— Sources**
      BT  Shakespeare, William, 1564-1616—
          Sources
Shakespeare, William, 1564-1616
- **— Acting**

Fig. 12. The beginning of the section on Shakespeare in *Library of Congress Subject Headings*, 22nd ed., 5 (5315).

might lead you to other pertinent works on your topic. *Griffin* allows you to search these subject headings directly from the entry for a book by clicking on the subject heading (underlined and sometimes highlighted in color). If you click on "Frontier and pioneer life in literature," you will find over fifty titles that match the heading. While many of these titles may not be pertinent, some of them may be useful.

Notice also that *Library of Congress Subject Headings* regularly supplies the general call numbers assigned to books and other library materials on given subjects. These numbers can be helpful for browsing. Although browsing can be productive, a random exploration of the bookshelves is no substitute for a systematic search of the catalog and appropriate reference sources. Some books related to your topic may be off the shelves when you browse, or they may be classified elsewhere. Most online catalogs like *Griffin* have a browsing feature that allows you to move from one entry to others with the same general call numbers. You can browse without fear of missing items that are currently in use. You can also save yourself some walking. In *Griffin*, you simply need to click on the call number (highlighted in blue) in any bibliographic record and you will find yourself in a list of library materials organized by call number. For example, if you click on the call number of the book by von Frank, the database shows you a list of other books next to it on the shelf (fig. 13). If you then click on any call number from this list, *Griffin* provides the corresponding bibliographic record and circulation status.

In addition to the features described earlier, many online catalogs provide ways to limit your search by language, material type (book, sound recording, etc.), publisher, year of publication, and location in the library system. This last limitation can be especially useful at large universities with many branch libraries. Such features can be helpful if you are searching a large database or if your search generates a long list of matches.

One additional tip on online catalogs that will be critical in the next chapter: some libraries do not catalog their journals or assign them a call number. Instead the journals are shelved alphabetically in a separate section devoted to periodicals. These journals may not be included in your online catalog but may be listed in a separate database, card file, or printed listing. Your reference librarian can tell you the convention chosen by your library.

| | | |
|---|---|---|
| | Ps 169 F7 S5 | |
| ☐ | The closed frontier; studies in American literary tragedy [b / **EWU JFK,WSU Holland** : | 1970 |
| | The closed frontier; studies in American literary tragedy [b / **EWU JFK,WSU Holland** : | 1970 |
| ☐ | Ps 169 F7 S65 1997 | |
| | Encyclopedia of frontier literature / Mary Ellen Snodgrass. / **WSU Holland** : | 1997 |
| ☐ | Ps 169 F7 V66 1985 | |
| | The sacred game : provincialism and frontier consciousness i / **WSU Holland** : | 1985 |
| | The sacred game : provincialism and frontier consciousness i / **WSU Holland** : | 1985 |
| ☐ | Ps 169 G66 D45 1995 | |
| | The death of Satan : how Americans have lost the sense of ev / **EWU JFK** : | 1995 |
| ☐ | Ps 169 G75 U78 1987 | |
| | The gruesome doorway : an analysis of the American grotesque / **WSU Holland** : | 1987 |
| ☐ | Ps 169 H4 G7 | |
| | The heroic ideal in American literature [by] Theodore L. Gro / **WSU Holland** : | 1971 |

Fig. 13. Entries for books classified near PS 169 F7 V66 1985, the call number for *The Sacred Game*, by Albert J. Von Frank, in *Griffin*.

Finally, be sure to confer with your reference librarian before you finish this step in your research. Your online catalog is, quite obviously, an extremely powerful research tool, one to which you will often return as you work on your term paper. The companies that produce the software for these online catalogs frequently offer new enhancements. *Griffin* may have many additional features by the time this book is published. Incidently, keep track of the subject headings and keywords you find most productive. Many of them will be equally useful when you search for essays in the next chapter.

# Moving beyond Your Library's Catalog

In the course of your research, you may discover that your library does not have all the books or periodicals that you want to read. As your research skills become more sophisticated, your need for materials not in your college library begins to mushroom.

Although some private colleges and universities do not open their libraries to nonaffiliated students, most academic libraries permit free use of their collections, provided that visitors do not remove any materials from the building. Some libraries in the same geographical area have even developed reciprocal borrowing privileges. Many state colleges and universities permit residents of the state to borrow books from their libraries for a small fee. Do not overlook the local public library. In some communities, particularly in large cities, the resources at the public library are more extensive than those in the local college library.

Since so many college and university libraries have made their online catalogs accessible over the Internet, you can often determine whether a trip to the neighboring library will be worthwhile before you even go there. Many libraries have created menus on their online catalogs that allow you to connect to the most commonly consulted library online catalogs in your state or region. Some libraries in the same state or region have created a union catalog by combining the bibliographic records from their online catalogs into a single database. If your library participates in such a consortium, it may be especially easy for you to see which titles are held by the other member libraries.

Your library may be able to borrow books and periodical articles for you from other libraries. The interlibrary loan process can take time, so begin your research early if you are likely to need materials from other libraries. In addition, many cooperative online catalogs permit users to request a book from another library directly online, bypassing the interlibrary loan department. It is important for you to familiarize yourself with library services that permit you to borrow materials from other libraries. Your reference librarian can best inform you of interlibrary loan policies, of any direct borrowing capabilities of your cooperative catalog, and of any reciprocal borrowing arrangements or other privileges available at nearby libraries.

All you need to consult the online catalog of another college or university is a microcomputer with access to the Internet. Most, if not all, colleges and university libraries have home pages—well-organized, easy-to-use online resources on their computer networks that let you choose from among a great variety of data resources, including library catalogs. Many libraries provide a direct link to the most commonly needed Web addresses for nearby libraries or for ones with which they have some consortial agreements. By clicking on this address, you go directly to the corresponding online catalog.

One of the most popular and comprehensive library catalogs is the

*Melvyl* database, a consolidated online catalog of the library holdings of the nine campuses of the University of California, the California State Library, the California Academy of Sciences, the California Historical Society, the Center for Research Libraries, and the Graduate Theological Union in Berkeley. *Melvyl* is the registered trademark of the Regents of the University of California and is part of the California Digital Library. The Web-based version of the *Melvyl* catalog can be reached at http://www.melvyl.ucop.edu/. With over 9 million unique titles representing 13.8 million holdings, this catalog provides an impressive database to augment your own library's holdings.

While similar in some ways to the *Griffin* catalog, the *Melvyl* catalog has many distinct features. If you are going to be consulting online library catalogs over the Internet, you will need to become comfortable teaching yourself how to use a variety of different systems with different searching capabilities. Through the use of the help commands and other information screens offered by these online catalogs, doing so can be easier than it might seem.

For example, if you click first on the banner labeled "Introduction" in the left side of the first screen and then on "Getting Started with the CAT and PE on the Web," you will find a brief but thorough description of the scope of the *Melvyl* catalog and the *California Periodicals Database* (fig. 14).

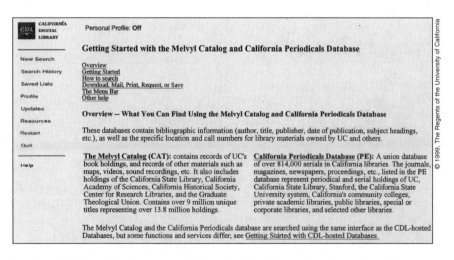

Fig. 14. "Getting Started" screen in the *Melvyl* database catalog from the University of California.

For our purposes, we will want to consult the *Melvyl* catalog. To give us some initial guidance, since we have not previously used this catalog, let's click on "Getting Started" and then "2. Search" in the section "How to Search" (fig. 15). Once again, *Melvyl* provides a brief but thorough description of the various features of this catalog, including the four types of searches—title, author, subject, and power. The power search permits the most sophisticated searching by combining terms and different search elements. In addition, you can limit your search by date, library location, and various other options (fig. 16).

To begin an author search, click on "New Search" in the column to the left and then "AUTHOR" under the search options. Notice that you can restrict your search to the entire catalog or to the last ten years. To find a book by Diane Gillespie, type the author's name in the space provided and then click on "Person" as opposed to "Organization" (fig.17). Six items match this author's name (fig.18). If you

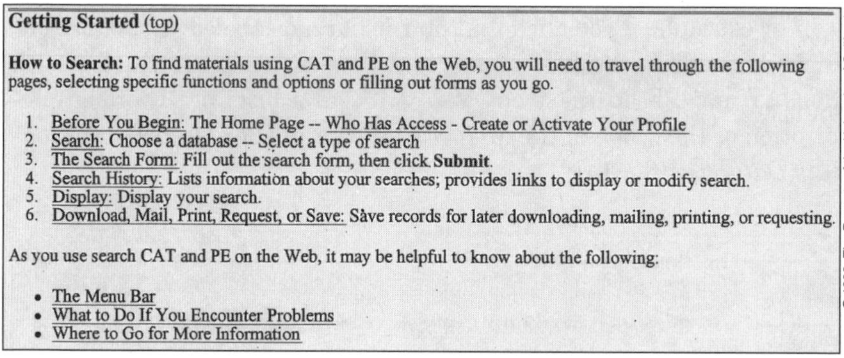

---

**Getting Started** (top)

**How to Search:** To find materials using CAT and PE on the Web, you will need to travel through the following pages, selecting specific functions and options or filling out forms as you go.

1. Before You Begin: The Home Page -- Who Has Access - Create or Activate Your Profile
2. Search: Choose a database -- Select a type of search
3. The Search Form: Fill out the search form, then click. **Submit**.
4. Search History: Lists information about your searches; provides links to display or modify search.
5. Display: Display your search.
6. Download, Mail, Print, Request, or Save: Save records for later downloading, mailing, printing, or requesting.

As you use search CAT and PE on the Web, it may be helpful to know about the following:

- The Menu Bar
- What to Do If You Encounter Problems
- Where to Go for More Information

---

Fig. 15. "How to Search" screen in the *Melvyl* catalog.

**Search (top)**

**First, choose a database:** Select either the Melvyl Catalog or the California Periodicals database from the pull-down menu.

Access to other CDL resources, including CDL-hosted databases also named in the "Choose a Database" pull-down menu, may be limited based upon license agreements and is explained in resource descriptions in the Directory of Collections and Services or in <u>Getting Started with CDL-hosted Databases</u>.

**Then, select a type of search:**

- **Title:** Search for materials by looking for significant words in the title or the exact beginning of the title. The search can be limited by library location, as well as by author, journal, or other options, depending on the database.
- **Author:** Search for materials by author (or by organization). This search can also be limited by library location, as well as by journal, an additional author, author affiliation, or other options, depending on the database.
- **Subject:** Search for materials by subject. Depending on the database you are searching, doing a Subject Search may allow you to search keywords in the title and subject headings. This screen also provides an **Alternate Strategies** link to suggestions on how best to locate works by subject. This search can also be limited by location.
- **Power:** You can to take full advantage of database search functions, including the ability to combine search terms using AND, OR, or NOT; to choose a number of different search types; and to apply the full range of limits to your search, including limits by date, library location, and other options, depending on the database.

Fig. 16. "Types of Searches" screen in the *Melvyl* catalog.

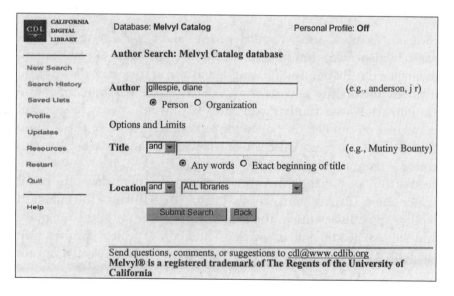

Fig. 17. Author search for Diane Gillespie in the *Melvyl* catalog.

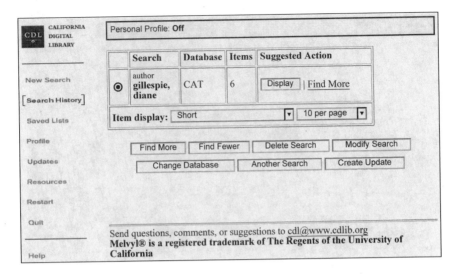

Fig. 18. Number of entries matching author search for Diane Gillespie in the *Melvyl* catalog.

click on "Display" you will retrieve the "short" display with all the basic bibliographic information—author, title, place of publication, publisher, date of publication, length and size of book. The display also includes universities and libraries, listed according to standard abbreviations, that own the book (fig. 19). If you face a very long list of matches, you can use the box to the left of each record to check those that interest you most. Once you have reviewed the whole list, you can create a more refined list of the items you checked. It is easy to proceed to the "long" display of a specific record by pulling down the menu under "Item Display" and choose "Long." In addition to the standard bibliographic information, the long display offers an item's language and subject headings along with a summary of which libraries own the book. Click on "All" in the holdings statement for the call numbers

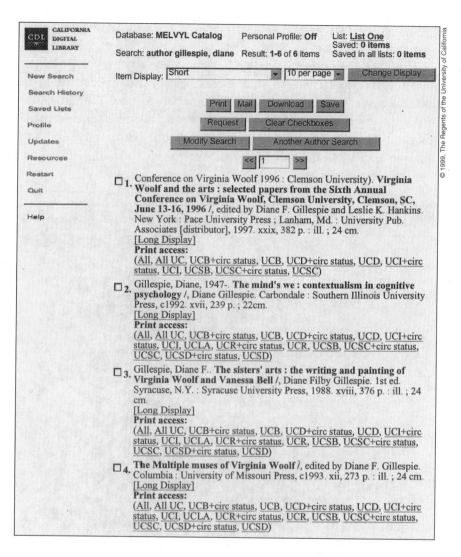

Fig. 19. Listing for the author Diane Gillespie in the *Melvyl* catalog.

and circulation status. Some of the *Melvyl* libraries offer circulation status; others do not (fig. 20).

By clicking on the appropriate box above the record, you can print your results, mail them to your e-mail account, download them to diskette, save them until you have compiled a more complete list, modify your search, begin another author search, and clear the checkboxes. To begin a totally new search, click on "New Search" in the upper left corner of the screen.

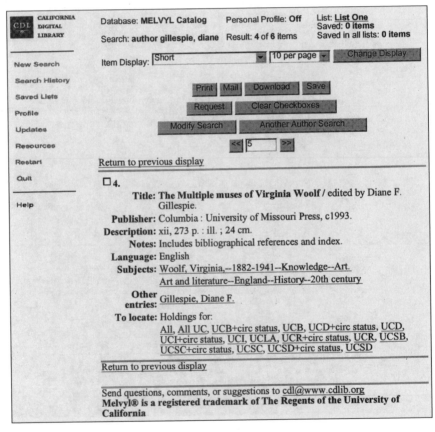

Fig. 20. Listing for *The Multiple Muses of Virginia Woolfe* in the *Melvyl* catalog.

If you try a title search, be aware that the database will match exact title or keywords in the title. Imagine that you are looking for a book entitled *Women, America, and Movement*. Although this book has a subtitle, you cannot remember it. If you ask the database to match "women, america, and movement" as keywords (i.e., "any words") in the title, you will get over twenty matches (fig. 21). However, if you specify that you want "exact title," you retrieve the one title that matches your request (fig. 22). In this instance, you have found exactly the book you need. If you had not retrieved the correct item, you would want to request the title as keyword, in case your recollection of the title was faulty. The formal Library of Congress subject headings for a known book on your topic can help you find other books on the same subject. For example, the book *Women, America, and Movement* is especially rich in subject headings that could lead to other useful books on pioneer life from the perspective of American women authors. Click on the subject heading "Frontier and pioneer life in literature" and you retrieve 134 matches. But many of these matches will not pertain to American women authors, the topic of your paper. By

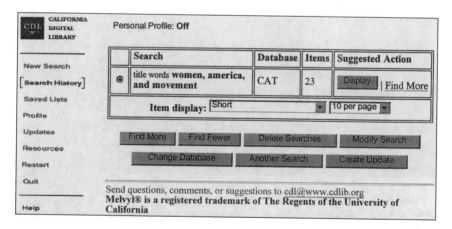

Fig. 21. Number of entries matching keywords in title search of *women, America, and movement* in the *Melvyl* catalog.

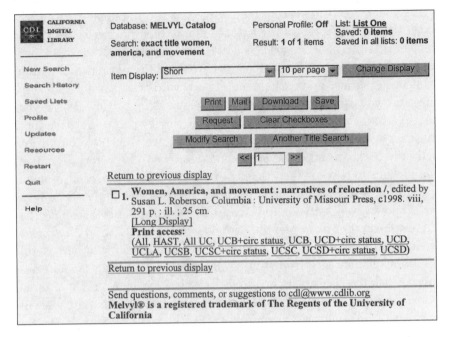

Fig. 22. Entry matching exact keywords in title for *women, America, and movement* in the *Melvyl* catalog.

combining the two most pertinent subject headings. "Frontier and pi-oneer life in literature" and "Women and Literature—United States—History," you discover several pertinent books (fig. 23).

The power search provides the greatest flexibility since you can combine a variety of characteristics and then limit the results by date, library location, language, and format of the publication. This capability is especially helpful when you are searching for a specific item with search terms that will likely retrieve hundreds of "hits" in such a large database. You can search by any combination of title words, exact title, subject, exact subject, personal author, corporate author, exact corporate author, conference, series, uniform title, international standard book number, and other characteristics. For example, assume that you had previously found a very useful book on Milton and wanted to find it again. Although you cannot remember the exact title, you know that "dissonance" and "images" were part of the title. In the *Melvyl* catalog, you can search for "milton, john" as subject words and combine this with the title words "dissonance" and "images." You can specify "books" as the format and limit your search to those books pub-

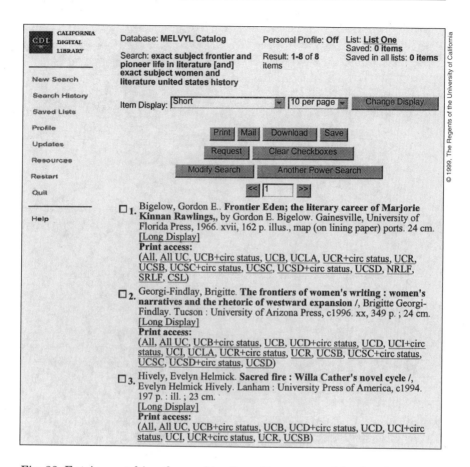

Fig. 23. Entries matching the combination of two exact subject headings in the *Melvyl* catalog.

lished during the last three years. This search matches one item in the database, a book entitled *Barbarous Dissonance and Images of Voice in Milton's Epics* (fig. 24). If this search had not identified the correct book, you would want to experiment more in case you were mistaken about the date of publication or some other aspect of the search.

Like all catalogs, there are many other features and tricks to *Melvyl*. Use the help screens throughout your searches. They are especially informative. Do not hesitate to ask your reference librarian for assistance in searching this database. Many libraries offer workshops on how to use online catalogs and other resources in English and American literature available over the Internet. Since information

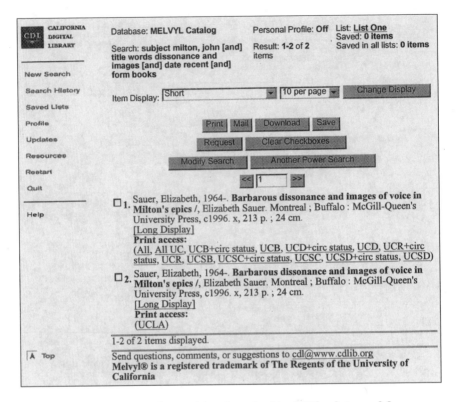

Fig. 24. Entry matching the combination of subject, title, date, and form search in the *Melvyl* catalog.

is increasingly being published in digital format, it is worth your time to take advantage of this instruction.

One last tip before we leave this chapter on books. As you search these catalogs, be on the lookout for a good bibliography on your topic. Such a book can reduce the possibility that you will overlook major studies. The Library of Congress uses the subheading "—Bibliography" after any formal subject heading to identify a published bibliography on that topic. Also, be sure to consult the list of references provided by the authors of the most useful books you locate through the online catalogs. These references can suggest important books and articles on your topic that you may otherwise miss.

Now that you have mastered two different online catalogs, *Griffin* and *Melvyl*, it is time to find articles.

# CHAPTER THREE

# Searching for Articles

A great deal of literary criticism appears in scholarly journals and in books of critical essays rather than in books written by one author. For this reason, it is vital that you search for periodical articles and essays on your topic. You may discover some helpful articles by looking at the bibliographies in the books you found on your topic. Then you need only determine whether your library owns the journals or books in which the articles are published. But even though you may have identified some articles through a bibliography for your topic, you should look for others by consulting an appropriate index or database.

Where you begin your search for scholarly articles on your topic depends on the scope of your project and on the availability of material. There is likely to be limited information on an author who has become prominent in the last decade or on a topic that is just beginning to receive attention. Established authors such as William Shakespeare or Emily Dickinson have been studied endlessly, resulting in an overwhelming amount of critical material. In these cases, it can be a challenge to sift through the many resources.

Identifying and locating articles on your topic may require significant perseverance, whether your topic has a little or a lot written on it. Research requires creativity as you evaluate the material you find and determine how it applies to your own research. You may not find an article precisely on your topic, and you may therefore need to think along broader or different lines, using different terminology.

A good starting point for researching many authors and their works is a series of publications that provide brief information about an author and then summarize some of the major criticism. Included among these are *Contemporary Literary Criticism, Nineteenth Century Literary Criticism, Black Literature Criticism, Poetry Criticism,* and *Short Story Criticism*. Many of these sources are available electronically through *Literature Resource Center*, which provides biographical and critical information about authors. Your library may subscribe to the electronic source or to some of the printed sets.

If you were looking for information on Sandra Cisneros's novel *The House on Mango Street, Contemporary Literary Criticism* would be a good starting point. There you would find an excerpt from an essay written by Julian Olivares called "Sandra Cisneros' *The House on Mango Street* and the Poetics of Space," published on pages 160–70 in a book of critical essays entitled *Chicana Creativity and Criticism: Charting New Frontiers in American Literature* (1988).

It is unlikely that one critical article will provide a range of perspectives about the book. An excellent source for locating articles in periodicals is the *Expanded Academic ASAP*, which covers the humanities, social sciences, and sciences. Libraries offer it on either CD-ROM or through the World Wide Web. This database contains some articles in their entirety and can be searched in a variety of ways, including by subject heading and keyword. The subject headings generally correspond to those found in *Library of Congress Subject Headings*, discussed in chapter 2.

When looking for a specific author and work, simply type the author's last name and part of the book title into the keyword box using the connector "and." To locate additional critical articles on Sandra Cisneros's *The House on Mango Street*, type the words "cisneros and mango" into the search box. This search retrieves references to, and some full texts of, eighteen periodical articles (fig. 25).

Identifying articles on themes in literature is much more challenging. It is generally preferable to begin with a keyword search. In the basic keyword search mode in *Expanded Academic ASAP*, the system will search for words in the titles, subject headings, authors, and summaries of the articles. For example, to locate articles on racial stereotypes in American literature, you would do a keyword search by typing the phrase "racial and stereotypes and american and litera-

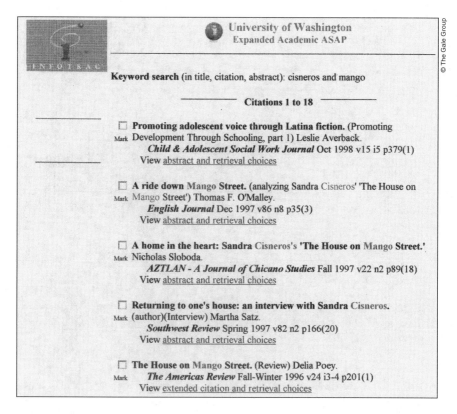

Fig. 25. Entries in *Expanded Academic ASAP* matching keywords *Cisneros* and *mango*.

ture." This search finds five articles, each having all four of these terms in the title, subject, article summary, or author. It is important to remember that the computer is quite literal about language. It looks only for the words exactly as they have been typed into the search box. This search needs to be redesigned because it seems likely that there are more than five articles on the topic.

Keyword searches require creative thought. Since you are not searching specific subject headings that bring different forms of a word together under one heading, you need to find out how to allow for the singular and plural forms of a word as well as for other forms of the root word. In this case, you would want to truncate to the root "rac" to pick up the words *races* and *racial* and to "stereotyp" to find *stereotypes* and *stereotypical* (fig. 26). The truncation, or wild card,

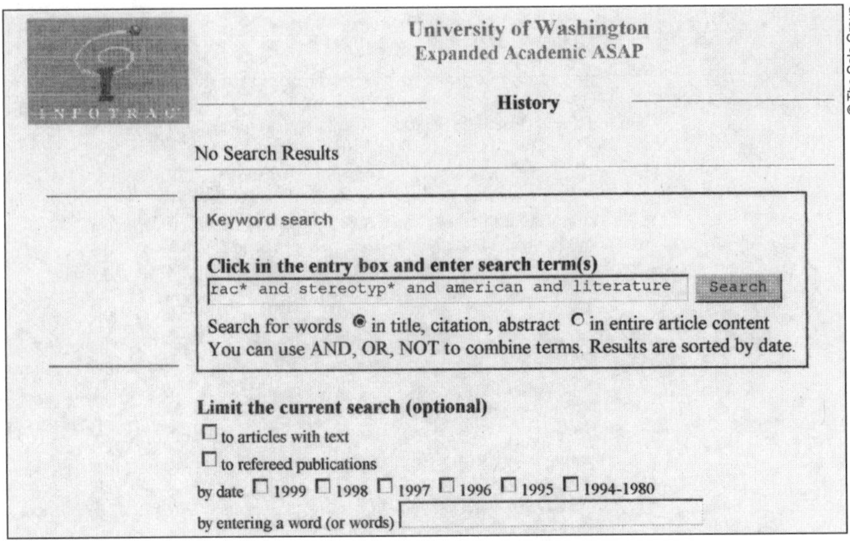

Fig. 26. Screen from *Expanded Academic ASAP* of keyword search using truncated words *rac* and *stereotyp* coupled with keywords *american* and *literature*.

symbol for this database and many others is the asterisk. The basic keyword search mode in *Expanded Academic ASAP* will search for these words in the titles, subject headings, authors, and summaries of the articles. In this type of search, the use of connector words (*and, or, not*) is especially important. The connector "and" narrows your search by limiting it to those records in which the terms connected by "and" are found in the same reference. The connector "or," used primarily to link synonyms, broadens your search and ensures that you retrieve all citations in which one or more of the synonyms is used. Instead of using the truncation symbol for "race," we could have typed in the words "race or races or racial." You may also decide to "or" this group with forms of the related word *ethnic*, which would retrieve additional references. Some databases offer an advanced search mode that works well for combining words using both "or" and "and" in the same search.

    This query of *Expanded Academic ASAP* for articles on racial stereotypes in American literature retrieves twenty references that match your search. Noting the article by Blewster in *Biblio* (fig. 27),

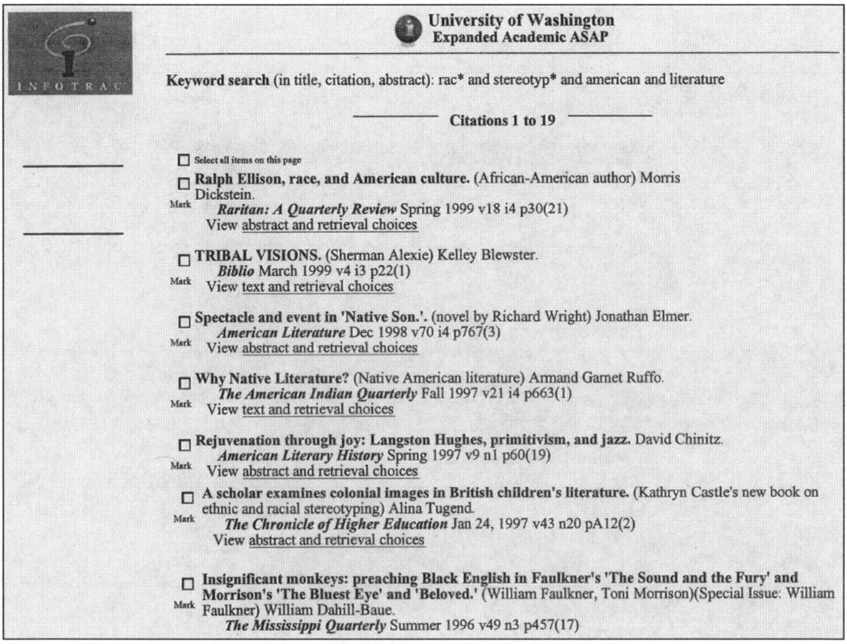

INFOTRAC

**University of Washington**
**Expanded Academic ASAP**

**Keyword search** (in title, citation, abstract): rac* and stereotyp* and american and literature

**Citations 1 to 19**

☐ Select all items on this page

☐ Mark **Ralph Ellison, race, and American culture.** (African-American author) Morris Dickstein.
***Raritan: A Quarterly Review*** Spring 1999 v18 i4 p30(21)
View abstract and retrieval choices

☐ Mark **TRIBAL VISIONS.** (Sherman Alexie) Kelley Blewster.
***Biblio*** March 1999 v4 i3 p22(1)
View text and retrieval choices

☐ Mark **Spectacle and event in 'Native Son.'.** (novel by Richard Wright) Jonathan Elmer.
***American Literature*** Dec 1998 v70 i4 p767(3)
View abstract and retrieval choices

☐ Mark **Why Native Literature?** (Native American literature) Armand Garnet Ruffo.
***The American Indian Quarterly*** Fall 1997 v21 i4 p663(1)
View text and retrieval choices

☐ Mark **Rejuvenation through joy: Langston Hughes, primitivism, and jazz.** David Chinitz.
***American Literary History*** Spring 1997 v9 n1 p60(19)
View abstract and retrieval choices

☐ Mark **A scholar examines colonial images in British children's literature.** (Kathryn Castle's new book on ethnic and racial stereotyping) Alina Tugend.
***The Chronicle of Higher Education*** Jan 24, 1997 v43 n20 pA12(2)
View abstract and retrieval choices

☐ Mark **Insignificant monkeys: preaching Black English in Faulkner's 'The Sound and the Fury' and Morrison's 'The Bluest Eye' and 'Beloved.'** (William Faulkner, Toni Morrison)(Special Issue: William Faulkner) William Dahill-Baue.
***The Mississippi Quarterly*** Summer 1996 v49 n3 p457(17)



Fig. 27. Listings retrieved by keyword search in *Expanded Academic ASAP* using truncated words *rac* and *stereotyp* along with keywords *american* and *literature*.

you decide to focus your attention on the works of Sherman Alexie. You can conduct a new search for pertinent articles about Alexie. Note that you can limit your search by adding words (fig. 28). By typing "rac*" (to include race, races, racial) or "ethnic*" (to include ethnic and ethnicity), you find two articles in addition to the one by Blewster (fig. 29). Scrolling to the end of one of these articles, you find links to other articles in the database on related subjects (fig. 30).

A citation in *Expanded Academic ASAP* includes author and title of the article, the name of the journal in which the article appears, the volume number, the page numbers, the date of publication, and usually a summary of the article. Note that all three articles on Sherman Alexie include the text, making it unnecessary in this case to find the actual periodicals.

Another good, general source for periodical articles is *Humanities Index*. Many libraries that do not subscribe to the *Expanded Academic*

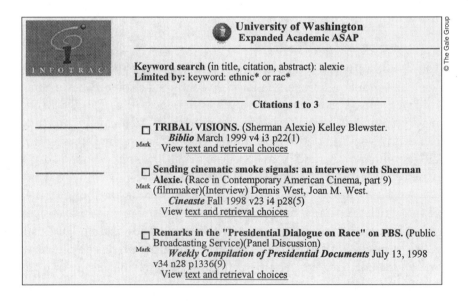

**University of Washington**
**Expanded Academic ASAP**

© The Gale Group

**History**

R2 ((alexie) and ke (ethnic* or rac*) ) (3 hits)
R1 (rac* and stereotyp* and american and literature) (20 hits)    [ View ]

**Keyword search**

**Click in the entry box and enter search term(s)**

[ alexie ]    [ Search ]

Search for words ⦿ in title, citation, abstract ◯ in entire article content
You can use AND, OR, NOT to combine terms. Results are sorted by date.

**Limit the current search (optional)**

☐ to articles with text
☐ to refereed publications
by date ☐ 1999 ☐ 1998 ☐ 1997 ☐ 1996 ☐ 1995 ☐ 1994-1980
by entering a word (or words) [ ethnic* or rac* ]

Fig. 28. Keyword search for *alexie* limited by truncated keywords *ethnic* and *rac* in *Expanded Academic ASAP*.

**University of Washington**
**Expanded Academic ASAP**

© The Gale Group

**Keyword search** (in title, citation, abstract): alexie
**Limited by:** keyword: ethnic* or rac*

**Citations 1 to 3**

☐ **TRIBAL VISIONS.** (Sherman Alexie) Kelley Blewster.
    *Biblio* March 1999 v4 i3 p22(1)
Mark   View text and retrieval choices

☐ **Sending cinematic smoke signals: an interview with Sherman**
    **Alexie.** (Race in Contemporary American Cinema, part 9)
Mark   (filmmaker)(Interview) Dennis West, Joan M. West.
    *Cineaste* Fall 1998 v23 i4 p28(5)
    View text and retrieval choices

☐ **Remarks in the "Presidential Dialogue on Race" on PBS.** (Public
    Broadcasting Service)(Panel Discussion)
Mark   *Weekly Compilation of Presidential Documents* July 13, 1998
    v34 n28 p1336(9)
    View text and retrieval choices

Fig. 29. The three entries matching keyword *alexie* and truncated keywords *ethnic* and *rac* coupled with keywords *american* and *literature* in *Expanded Academic ASAP*.

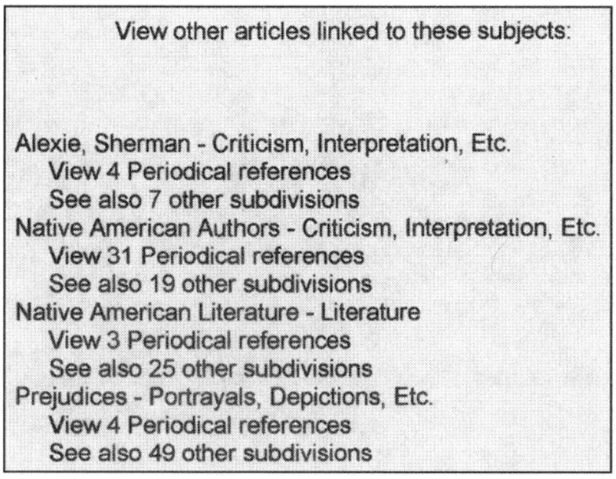

View other articles linked to these subjects: © The Gale Group

Alexie, Sherman - Criticism, Interpretation, Etc.
    View 4 Periodical references
    See also 7 other subdivisions
Native American Authors - Criticism, Interpretation, Etc.
    View 31 Periodical references
    See also 19 other subdivisions
Native American Literature - Literature
    View 3 Periodical references
    See also 25 other subdivisions
Prejudices - Portrayals, Depictions, Etc.
    View 4 Periodical references
    See also 49 other subdivisions

Fig. 30. "Other articles linked to these subjects" in *Expanded Academic ASAP.*

*ASAP* may provide access to *Humanities Index* in electronic or book format. Most of the periodicals indexed in *Humanities Index* are also in the *Expanded Academic ASAP.* Your library may offer *Humanities Index* on CD-ROM or through a Web-based online service from OCLC called *FirstSearch*.

Let's try a search on the depiction of women in *Hamlet* using *Humanities Index* (called *Humanities Abstracts* in *FirstSearch*). The introductory menu offers you the choice of searching by author, subject, or title, with subject as the default search. A subject search will retrieve all citations for the terms you provide as long as these terms are found either in the subject headings or as keywords in the title of the article. A search using the terms "Hamlet" and "women" gives you a list of thirteen pertinent articles (fig. 31). By clicking on the underlined titles, you will receive complete citations along with summaries or abstracts for more recent articles.

One special feature of *FirstSearch* is its listing of libraries that are known to own various journals. In figure 32, notice that one of our libraries, the University of Washington, is indicated as owning *Mosaic*. If your library does not appear to own the item, that sentence will read "Ownership: Check the catalogs in your library." In fact, it is important to check your own catalog since some libraries do not list all their journals in the *FirstSearch* database. In addition, your catalog will provide the local call number or location for that journal in your library. You can also see who else has the journal by clicking on the box at either the top or the bottom of the *FirstSearch* screen labeled "Libraries with Item." It should be possible to obtain the article you

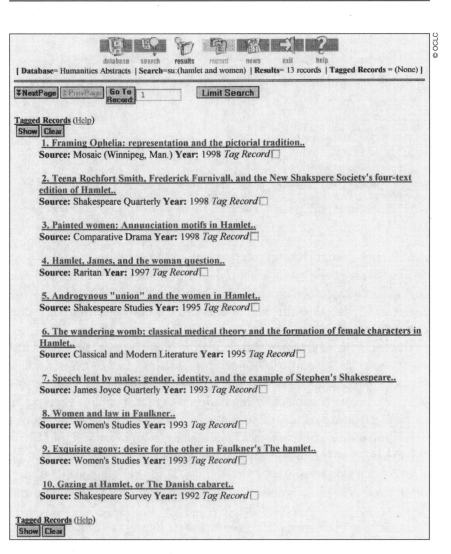

Fig. 31. Listing of entries matching keywords *hamlet* and *women* in *Humanities Abstracts* on *FirstSearch*.

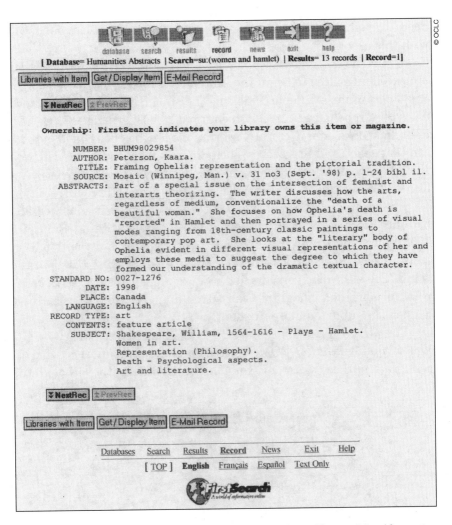

Fig. 32. Library ownership statement in a record from *Humanities Abstracts* on *FirstSearch*.

need through interlibrary loan. A reference librarian can help you with this process.

While the *Expanded Academic Index* and the *Humanities Index* are excellent places to begin the search for articles, they cover only a small part of the available criticism. The *MLA Bibliography* is a much more comprehensive source with citations to books, articles in periodicals and books, and doctoral dissertations for the entire field of modern languages and literatures, including English and American. You should be aware that as a general rule most college and university libraries do not collect doctoral dissertations from other universities.

The printed volumes of the *MLA Bibliography* from 1922 to 1955 list only literary criticism published in the United States. But since 1955, the bibliography has become increasingly international in scope; it now indexes books and periodicals published throughout the world. The electronic versions list articles published since 1963. In its print format, the bibliography is issued annually, while the electronic versions are updated more frequently.

The *MLA Bibliography* may be available in your library on the World Wide Web or CD-ROM. Several database companies provide access. Each of these electronic versions works differently, although the

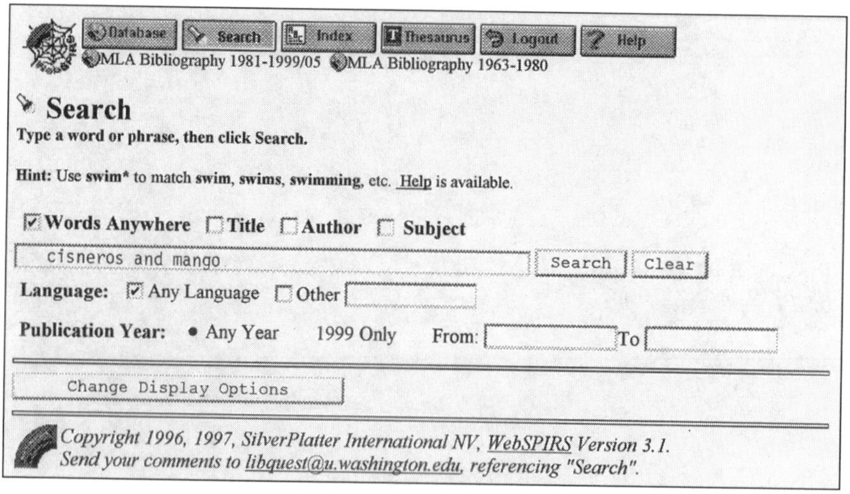

Fig. 33. Keyword search of *Cisneros* and *mango* in the *MLA Bibliography on* SilverPlatter *WebSPIRS 3.1.*

**Search History**

#1 **cisneros and mango** (*44 records*)

**TI**
    Teaching Contemporary American Ethnic Women's Literature: Literary and Extra-Literary Traditions
**AU**
    Grobman,-Laurie-Ellen
**SO**
    Dissertation-Abstracts-International,-Section-A:-The-Humanities-and-Social-Sciences, Ann Arbor, MI (DAIA). 1998 May, 58:11, 4270 DAI No.: DA9814963. Degree granting institution: Lehigh U, 1998
**AN**
    98083268

**TI**
    Beyond the Private Sphere: Writing as Space of Self-Affirmation in Martin Gaite, Esquivel and Cisneros
**AU**
    Lago-Grana-Pearson,-Josefa
**SO**
    Dissertation-Abstracts-International,-Section-A:-The-Humanities-and-Social-Sciences, Ann Arbor, MI (DAIA). 1998 May, 58:11, 4266 DAI No.: DA9815896. Degree granting institution: U of Nebraska, Lincoln, 1997
**AN**
    98083253

    Back to Record Display

Fig. 34. Listing for two dissertations matching the keyword search *Cisneros* and *mango* in the *MLA Bibliography* on SilverPlatter *WebSPIRS 3.1.*

basic search features are similar. Our example will use the Silver-Platter *WebSPIRS* version. Recall that a search of *Expanded Academic ASAP* for articles on Sandra Cisneros's *The House on Mango Street* turned up eighteen articles. Perhaps only a few of those were useful to your research. Combining "cisneros" and "mango" in the *MLA Bibliography* search box finds forty-four references in the database (fig. 33). Glancing through the first few references, you see that several of them are for dissertations (fig. 34). To find critical articles in periodicals or in books, you can return to the original search screen to

---

**Search History**

   #3 **#1 and #2** (*32 records* )
   #2 ((ARTICLE in PT) or (BOOK-ARTICLE in PT) or (JOURNAL-ARTICLE in PT) ) and
   (english in la ) (*769336 records* )
   #1 cisneros and mango (*44 records* )

---

Usage is subject to the terms and conditions of the subscription and License Agreement and the
applicable Copyright and intellectual property protection as dictated by the appropriate laws of your
country and/or International Convention.

Copyright Information

---

**TI**
      The 'Wild Zone' Thesis as Gloss in Chicana Literary Study
**AU**
      Candelaria,-Cordelia-Chavez
**SO**
      248-56 IN Warhol-Robyn-R. (ed. and introd.); Herndl-Diane-Price (ed. and introd.). Feminisms:
An Anthology of Literary Theory and Criticism. New Brunswick, NJ : Rutgers UP, 1997. xxi, 1207 pp.
**AN**
      97077724

---

      Back to Record Display

---

Fig. 35. Listing of book matching a search for *Cisneros* and *mango*, limited to
articles and books in English from the *MLA Bibliography* on SilverPlatter
*WebSPIRS 3.1.*

limit your search to those types of publications. Since the *MLA
Bibliography* includes articles in all languages, you might also want to
limit your search to only those languages you read. By removing dissertations and articles in languages other than English, your list now
has thirty-two references. One of the first references lists an article
published in a book edited by an author other than the one who wrote
the article (fig. 35). This is important since neither the author nor the
title of the article is likely to be listed in your library's catalog. You will
need to look up the editor of the book (Warhol) or the title of the book
(*Feminisms: An Anthology of Literary Theory and Criticism*). Note
that the *MLA Bibliography* currently does not provide summaries or
full texts of the articles listed. Some of the journals you need may be
available electronically through your library, but most will probably
still be in print format. Another helpful feature of the *MLA Bibliography* is the *Thesaurus*, which is a list of the subject headings used
in the database. As with most databases, the *MLA Bibliography* al-

lows you to change how much of the citation you display, and you can e-mail the search results to yourself. It is always a good idea to take advantage of the "help" option to learn how best to search the database, especially since features and options are enhanced on a frequent basis.

Essays within books are generally not listed in library catalogs and are only covered selectively by the *MLA Bibliography*, yet they are a valuable source of literary criticism. The *Essay and General Literature Index,* published since 1934, cites essays and chapters in books in the humanities, social sciences, and natural sciences. Though far from comprehensive, it can direct you to discussions of specific subjects that are buried in more general collections. Your library may have the print edition or provide access to an electronic version of *Essay and General Literature Index.*

Searching electronic indexes is normally faster and more efficient than using a printed source. The ability to link together a number of keywords focuses the electronic search in a way that simply is not possible with printed indexes, which permit you to consult only one term at a time. Electronic indexes also allow you to search many years at once instead of one year at a time. If your library does not subscribe to the electronic indexes discussed here, be sure to ask your reference librarian if a suitable alternative is available. There are other electronic indexes covering English and American literature. In addition, you may still need to check a print index if you are looking for older articles. Most electronic indexes, especially those offering full text, go back no earlier than the mid-1980s.

There are other useful printed and electronic resources covering English and American literature, including the *Annual Bibliography for English Studies*, a Web database indexing articles from periodicals and books. This is more selective in coverage than the *MLA Bibliography* but is another good place to start a search. The growing interdisciplinary nature of studies in English and American literature may require that you seek scholarly articles in other disciplines such as art, history, or psychology. For example, an examination of racial and ethnic issues in American literature would benefit from a search of the sociology database *Sociological Abstracts,* and any topic with psychological overtones may require a search of *PsycInfo*, the database of articles in psychology.

CHAPTER FOUR

# Finding Book Reviews

There may not be much literary criticism on a recently published work; the only treatment of such a work may be a book review in a current (perhaps even popular) periodical or newspaper. For such criticism you can consult indexes to book reviews.

The *Expanded Academic ASAP*, which we discussed in chapter 3, also indexes book reviews from the periodicals it covers. For example, using "and" to combine the phrase "reservation blues" with the publication type "reviews," you will find seven reviews of *Reservation Blues,* a novel by Sherman Alexie, in the online *Expanded Academic ASAP* (fig. 36). Note that you can view the text for the third item, the review by Leslie Marmon Silko in the *Nation* (fig. 37). Others, such as the first one from the *Prairie Schooner*, provide only the citation to the review. You will need to consult your library catalog to find out whether your library subscribes to these periodicals.

Even if your library does not offer access to the *Expanded Academic ASAP*, it most likely will have the two major indexes to book reviews—*Book Review Digest* and *Book Review Index*. Both have printed and electronic versions. Our illustrations are taken from the printed versions. Although the *Digest* began publication in 1905, sixty years earlier than the *Index*, its coverage is much more limited than that of its younger rival. Before any review for a work of fiction is listed in *Book Review Digest*, at least three reviews of the book must have been published in the periodicals indexed. Before 1991, fiction had to have

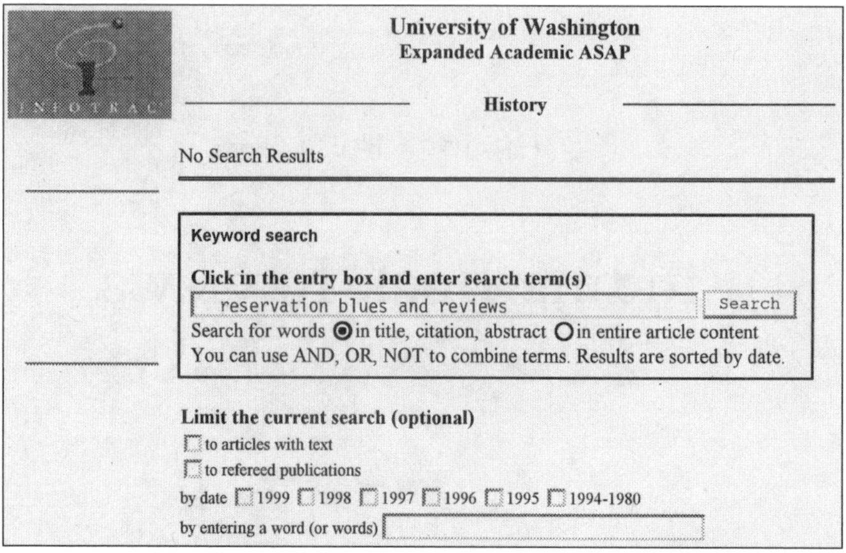

Fig. 36. Search for book reviews of *Reservation Blues* in *Expanded Academic ASAP*.

been reviewed at least four times. At the same time, *Book Review Digest* is very up-to-date, published quarterly with annual cumulations. The *Digest*'s editors sometimes furnish brief excerpts from the more important reviews, and they provide word counts so that you know whether a review is simply a short paragraph or a substantial essay. If, for example, you were looking for criticism of *Reservation Blues*, the 1996 volume of *Book Review Digest* lists six book reviews in a variety of publications. The fourth review, from the *New York Times Book Review*, is a good example of the kind of summary *Book Review Digest* frequently provides (fig. 38). Notice that the review is substantial, 1,200 words in length. A list of the abbreviations for the periodicals indexed is supplied at the front of each volume (fig. 39). To find this review, you need to consult your library's catalog to determine whether your library subscribes to these periodicals.

Although *Book Review Index* does not provide excerpts from reviews, it indexes more periodicals than either *Book Review Digest* or

**University of Washington**
**Expanded Academic ASAP**

**Keyword search** (in title, citation, abstract): reservation blues and reviews

**Citations 1 to 7**

☐ **Reservation Blues.** (book reviews) Lee Lemon.
Mark ***Prairie Schooner*** Spring 1996 v70 n1 p185(2)
View extended citation and retrieval choices

☐ **Reservation Blues.** (book reviews) Frederick Busch.
Mark ***The New York Times Book Review*** July 15, 1995 p9 col 1 (17 col in)
View extended citation and retrieval choices

☐ **Reservation Blues.** (book reviews) Leslie Marmon Silko.
Mark ***The Nation*** June 12, 1995 v260 n23 p856(4)
View text and retrieval choices

☐ **Reservation Blues.** (book reviews) Bill Ott.
Mark ***Booklist*** June 1, 1995 v91 n19-20 p1726(1)
View text and retrieval choices

☐ **Reservation Blues.** (book reviews) David Sowd.
Mark ***Library Journal*** June 1, 1995 v120 n10 p158(1)
View extended citation and retrieval choices

☐ **Reservation Blues.** (book reviews) Pam Lambert.
Mark ***People Weekly*** May 8, 1995 v43 n18 p35(1)
View text and retrieval choices

☐ **Reservation Blues.** (book reviews)
Mark ***Publishers Weekly*** May 1, 1995 v242 n18 p42(2)
View text and retrieval choices



Fig. 37. Listing of entries for book reviews of *Reservation Blues* in *Expanded Academic ASAP*.

*Expanded Academic ASAP*. In addition, *Book Review Index* sets no minimum number of reviews as a criterion for inclusion. To be listed, a book need only have been reviewed in one of the periodicals covered. A quick check of the 1995 volume of *Book Review Index* lists a few additional reviews for *Reservation Blues*, including one in *Bloomsbury Review* (figs. 40a and b). Since 1969, *Book Review Index* has also been available online through *Dialog*.

**ALEXIE, SHERMAN, 1966-.** Reservation blues. 306p $21 1996
Warner Bks.
    ISBN 0-446-67235-1    LC 96-33838

SUMMARY: This novel tells the story "of Coyote Springs, an all
Indian-Catholic 'four-and-a-half chord' rock band formed after a
chance encounter with . . . Delta bluesman Robert Johnson, who
happens onto the Spokane Indian Reservation looking for the
woman in his dreams to save him from the mysterious 'Gentleman' [Devil] on his trail." (Libr J)

REVIEW: *Booklist* v91 p1726 Je 1-15 '95. Bill Ott (280w)

REVIEW: *Libr J* v120 p158 Je 1 '95. David Sowd (160w)
    "A 29-year-old Spokane/Coeur d'Alene Indian whose 1993
collection of stories, The Lone Ranger and Tonto Fistfight in
Heaven, won a PEN/Hemingway Award citation for best first
book of fiction, Alexie continues in the same mythopoetic vein
with this remarkable first novel. . . . Like the Native American
trickster figure from whom this unlikely ensemble borrows its
name, the narrative surprises at every turn, transcending the familiar tragedy of reservation life with humor and lyricism. Highly recommended."

REVIEW: *MultiCult Rev* v5 p61 Je '96. Joel Monture (310w)

REVIEW: *N Y Times Book Rev* p9 Jl 16 '95. Frederick Busch
    (1200w)
    "[The author] catches the ancient and the contemporary, the
solemn and the self-mocking, at once; he evokes dreary days of
watching black-and-white television reruns in a place of 'poverty,
suicide, alcoholism.' . . . When Mr. Alexie writes at his best, he
creates stinging commentary. . . . When he goes wrong, it is because he tries to suggest that a rock band can bear the metaphori-
cal weight of an entire culture—not even Roddy Doyle's novel
'The Commitments' sustained such a concept. . . . Though there
is wonderful humor and profound sorrow in this novel, and bril-
liant renditions of each, there is not enough structure to carry the
dreams and tales that Mr. Alexie needs to portray and that we
need to read. His talent may be for the short form. But the talent
is real, and it is very large, and I will gratefully read whatever
he writes, in whatever form."

REVIEW: *Nation* v260 p856 Je 12 '95. Leslie Marmon Silko
    (2450w)
    "Unlike the bucolic idylls of small-town America pawned off
by, say, Garrison Keillor, Alexie's portrayal of the reservation
town of Well-pinit and its people is in the tradition of communities evoked in The Scarlet Letter, Babbitt, Sanctuary and The
Last Picture Show. These small towns are like the old cat who
eats her kittens. . . . Alexie's talent is immense and genuine.
. . . The power of his writing rises out of the Spokane River and
the Spokane earth where it is sweetened with the music of Robert Johnson, Hank Williams, Elvis Presley, Janis Joplin and Jimi
Hendrix. On this big Indian reservation we call 'the United
States,' Sherman Alexie is one of the best writers we have."

REVIEW: *World Lit Today* v70 p446 Spr '96. Howard Meredith
    (600w)
    "Form and content act in unity to provide a captivating story
of the tragic sense of life within a Spokane frame of reference.
. . . Reservation Blues provides an intimate perception of Spokane tribal tenets and mood within a multicultural frame of reference. Death, alcohol, poverty, book-burning, and child abuse find
their place, along with a sense of the land and the search for tradition. . . . Each character provides added richness to the community in which the story is set. . . . Sherman Alexie invites us
to participate in this extraordinary work of art, which serves as
a healing process."

Fig. 38. Listing of book reviews of *Reservation Blues* in
*Book Review Digest 1996* (34).

```
                              N

N Engl Q — The New England Quarterly
N Y Rev Books — The New York Review of Books
N Y Times Book Rev — The New York Times Book Review
Nat Hist — Natural History
Nation — The Nation
Natl Rev — National Review
New Leader — The New Leader
New Repub — The New Republic
New Sci — New Scientist
New Statesman (Engl) — New Statesman (London, England:
    1996)
New Statesman Soc — New Statesman & Society
New Yorker — The New Yorker
Newsweek — Newsweek
Notes — Notes
```

Fig. 39. Abbreviations used for the periodicals indexed
in *Book Review Digest 1996.*

```
Alexie, Sherman - The Business of Fancydancing
     APR - v24 - Jl '95 - p29+ [501+]
Coyote Spring
     LJ - v119 - O 15 '94 - p72 [1-50]
First Indian on the Moon
     APR - v24 - Jl '95 - p29+ [501+]
     WAL - v29 - Fall '94 - p277+ [501+]
The Lone Ranger and Tonto Fistfight in Heaven
     APR - v24 - Jl '95 - p29+ [501+]
  y  Kliatt - v29 - Ja '95 - p4 [51-250]
     NYTBR - v99 - O 16 '94 - p44 [1-50]
     WAL - v29 - Fall '94 - p277+ [501+]
     WER - Fall '95 - p57 [51-250]
Old Shirts and New Skins
     WAL - v29 - Fall '94 - p277+ [501+]
Reservation Blues
  y  BL - v91 - Je 1 '95 - p1726 [51-250]
  y  BL - v91 - Je 1 '95 - p1741 [1-50]
     Bloom Rev - v15 - Jl '95 - p16 [501+]
     HMR - Sum '95 - p22 [251-500]
     HMR - Sum '95 - p24+ [501+]
     KR - v64 - Mr 15 '95 - p324 [251-500]
     LATBR - Je 18 '95 - p2+ [501+]
     LJ - v120 - Je 1 '95 - p158 [51-250]
     Nat - v260 - Je 12 '95 - p856+ [501+]
     NYTBR - v100 - Jl 16 '95 - p9+ [501+]
     PW - v242 - My 1 '95 - p42+ [51-250]
```

Fig. 40a. Listing of book reviews of
*Reservation Blues* by Sherman Alexie in
*Book Review Index 1995* (13).

```
Bloom Rev: Bloomsbury Review
Bimonthly   ISSN 0276-1564
1762 Emerson St.
Denver, CO 80218
```

Fig. 40b. Abbreviations
and full names of first periodical listed under
*Reservation Blues* in *Book
Review Index 1995* (xii).

*Research Library Periodicals*, a *ProQuest* database, indexes a number of periodicals that publish book reviews. In this database, it is necessary to search the current file (1997–present, as of this writing) separately from the back file, which covers 1986–96. Since *Reservation Blues* appeared in 1995, try searching the back file first. It is best to use the advanced search feature to find book reviews because it allows you to limit your search. Enter the phrase "reservation blues" in the first search box, then move down to the box labeled "in Article Type" and change the setting from "ALL" to "book review" by using the pull-down feature. At the bottom of the screen, again using the pull-down feature, change the date range from "Current" to "Backfile" (fig. 41). This identifies thirteen reviews of *Reservation Blues*. Notice the graphic of a page in the fourth column of the second listing (fig. 42). This indicates that you can retrieve the full text of the review from the *World Literature Today* database. By clicking the mouse on that graphic, you can see the citation and the complete review (fig. 43).

Of course, indexes to book reviews also compile reviews of nonfiction. These commentaries can indicate how a book of criticism was

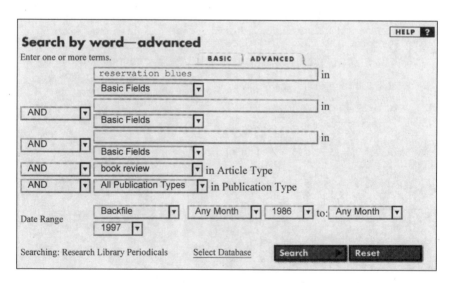

Fig. 41. Screen for an advanced word search for book reviews of *Reservation Blues* in *Research Library Periodicals* in *ProQuest*.

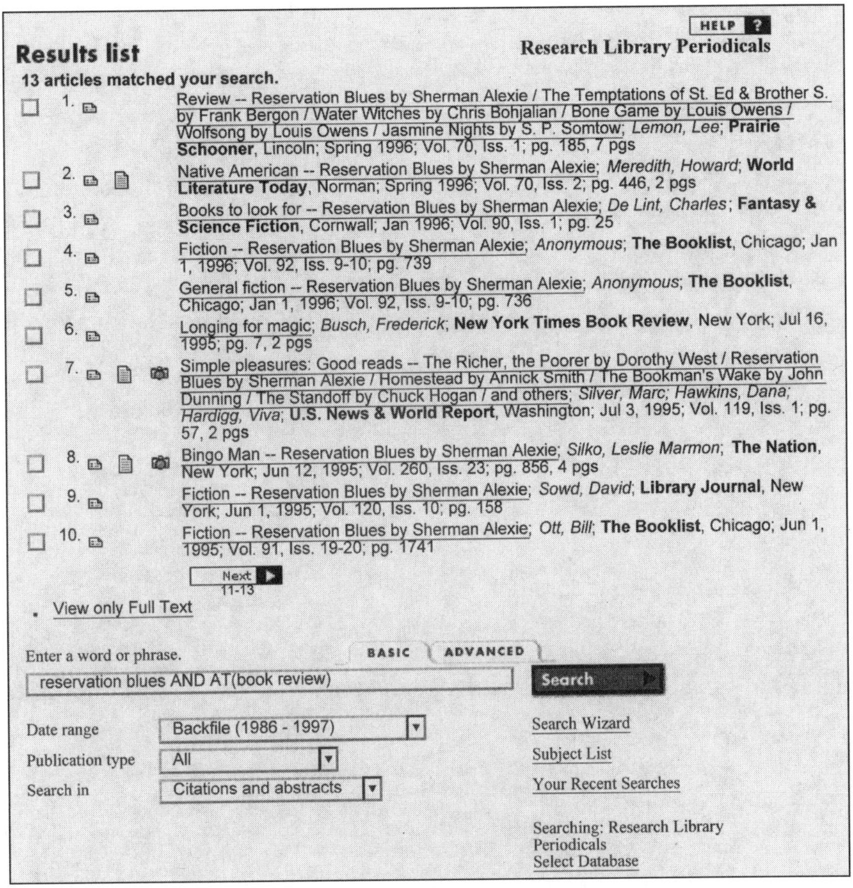

Fig. 42. Listing of full-text book reviews for *Reservation Blues* in *Research Library Periodicals* in *ProQuest*.

received at the time of its publication. Assume you are preparing a paper on gender in Shakespeare and were planning to use Linda Bamber's *Comic Women, Tragic Men: A Study of Gender and Genre in Shakespeare* (Stanford UP, 1982). You might want to read reviews of this study to learn what other Shakespearean scholars think of it. While *Expanded Academic ASAP, Book Review Index, Book Review Digest*, and *ProQuest* can supply some citations, two other indexes might be better suited to this kind of research problem. An *Index to Book Reviews in the Humanities*, because it indexes reviews from over

**Native American -- Reservation Blues by Sherman Alexie** `HELP ?`
*World Literature Today*; Norman; Spring 1996; Meredith, Howard;

| | |
|---|---|
| **Volume:** | 70 |
| **Issue:** | 2 |
| **Start Page:** | 446 |
| **ISSN:** | 01963570 |
| **Subject Terms:** | Novels |
| **Abstract:** | |

*Review.*

**Full Text:**
*Copyright University of Oklahoma Spring 1996*

Sherman Alexie. Reservation Blues. New York. Atlantic Monthly. 1995. 306 pages. $21. ISBN 0-87113-594-9.

The art of Sherman Alexie surprises and delights the reader as the dreamlike images and hard-edged realities in Reservation Blues find a center on the Spokane Indian Reservation. Form and content act in unity to provide a captivating story of the tragic sense of life within a Spokane frame of reference. This beautifully written vision of the earth invites participation in specific patterns of existence.

Reservation Blues provides an intimate perception of Spokane tribal tenets and mood within a multicultural frame of reference. Death, alcohol, poverty, book-burning, and child abuse find their place, along with a sense of the land and the search for tradition. Thomas Builds-the-Fire speaks in a dream sequence for the community when he says, "Maybe something bad is going to happen to us if we don't have something better on our mind." Each character provides added richness to the community in which the story is set, from the Warm Water sisters Chess and Checkers, to Big Mom the Spokane medicine woman, to Robert Johnson the magnificent blues guitarist.

Thomas loves the land. The reservation provides structural support even in its reduced state: "The reservation was gone itself, just a shell of its former self, just a fragment of the whole. But the reservation still possessed power and rage, magic and loss, joys and jealousy. The reservation tugged at the lives of its Indians, stole from them in the middle of the night, watched impassively as the horses and salmon disappeared. But the reservation forgave, too." This spatial and temporal presence offers a solid sense of place.

Spiritual themes run throughout the novel, reflecting material and ethereal concerns of power and peace. The interior life of the principal characters is offered in their dreams and their thoughts as they are carried along by forces over which they have little or no control. Each passing moment is imbued with a strong sense of the past and future, but rarely in a sequential fashion. Cause-and-effect progressions lose their sense of direction in Alexie's artistic design and native images. The metaphors of tribal song and dance are offered as the structural pattern for understanding the layered nature of existence, even to the point when, as Alexie writes, "I think God loves to dance as much as the rest of us."

Songs and repetitions of sounds call our attention to the rhythms of the peoples' lives. Their echoes in the text reinforce attention to the importance of the words and underline the points of the traditional sense of life patterns. Alexie's wordplay contributes to meaning, emphasizing unity in the multiplicity of the impact of cultural forces upon the lives of the Spokane Indian community. In the end, which is also a beginning, Alexie writes: "In a dream, Chess, Checkers, and Thomas sat at the drum with Big Mom during the powwow. All the Spokane Indians crowded around the drum, too. They all pounded the drum and sang. Big Mom taught them a new song, the shadow horses' song, the slaughtered horses' song, the screaming horses' song, a song of mourning that would become a song of celebration: we have survived, we have survived." Sherman Alexie invites us to participate in this extraordinary work of art, which serves as a healing process.

Fig. 43. Citation and beginning of the full text of the review of *Reservation Blues* published by *World Literature Today* in *Research Library Periodicals* in *ProQuest.*

seven hundred scholarly journals, is far more likely to pick up erudite evaluations of serious studies like Bamber's. Since this index ceased publication with the 1990 volume, however, it will only prove useful if the critical work was published between 1960 and 1990.

A second choice might be the *Annual Bibliography of English Language and Literature*, which was mentioned briefly in the last chapter. Since the bibliography notes book reviews of critical works in its entries for those works, it would be another logical place to look for reviews of Bamber's study. By the way, *Humanities Index*, discussed in the previous chapter, includes book reviews in the online versions and lists them in the final section of each printed issue.

CHAPTER FIVE

# Finding Supplementary Information: Other Reference Sources

## Biographical Sources

For most undergraduate term papers, you may not need biographical information on the authors studied in the course or on the critics who wrote about them. But occasionally a few biographical facts can shed additional light on an author's work or on a research problem. Many reference books discuss the lives of English and American writers. Some supply only a brief paragraph or two of basic data—dates and places of birth and death, major works, and the like. Others offer lengthy treatments of each author's life and literary accomplishments.

The *Dictionary of Literary Biography (DLB)* is one of the best examples of a comprehensive literary dictionary that merges factual information and critical opinion. This huge set is kept up to date through the publication of yearbooks. Each volume is devoted to a different genre or literary period covering North American and many other literatures and contains biographical essays, each written by a different scholar. A cumulative index to the entire set to date appears in the back of each volume. In other words, you need only consult the final index to determine which volume covers the author you seek.

Authors who have written in more than one genre will usually have essays appearing in more than one volume and written by different scholars. For example, there is an essay on Robert Penn Warren in volume 2, *American Novelists since World War II*, and volume 48, *American Poets, 1880–1945*. Furthermore, there is an updated entry on Warren in the 1980 yearbook. The 1989 yearbook includes an eleven-page obituary for Warren, written by Victor Strandberg, of Duke University, who also wrote the entry on Warren in volume 48. If you were interested in Warren as a poet, the essay in volume 48, supplemented by the two in the yearbooks, would clearly be more informative than the essay in volume 2. If you were interested in Warren as a talented author of several genres, you might want to consult all four entries.

As another example, if you needed background on George Eliot, the index would direct you to volume 21, *Victorian Novelists before 1885*. The twenty-six-page entry for Eliot begins with basic biographical information—that is, birth, marriage, and death dates as well as a bibliography of primary works. What follows is an excellent critical essay on Eliot's literary contributions, written by Joseph Wiesenfarth, of the University of Wisconsin. The *DLB* is also a good place to find a photograph or sketch of the author since most entries, especially those for the more prominent authors, are well illustrated (fig. 44).

Large and definitive, authoritative and readable, the *Dictionary of National Biography (DNB)*, edited by Leslie Stephens and Sidney Lee, describes the lives and work of British writers as well as those of Britons famous in other occupations. The length of each biographical account is proportionate to the importance of the subject. Shakespeare is awarded forty-nine pages, Keats only fifteen. The equivalent of the *DNB* on this side of the Atlantic is the *Dictionary of American Biography (DAB)*. Like its British counterpart, the *DAB* discusses at some length prominent deceased Americans of all professions. Critics of the *DAB* have lamented that many distinguished American women are absent from its pages. In fact, *Notable American Women (NAW)*, a four-volume companion to the *DAB*, has been published specifically to

Basic biographical information

# George Eliot
## (Mary Ann Evans)

Joseph Wiesenfarth
*University of Wisconsin*

BIRTH: South Farm, Arbury, Warwickshire, 22
November 1819, to Robert and Christiana Pearson
Evans.

MARRIAGE: 6 May 1880 to John Walter Cross.

DEATH: London, 22 December 1880.

BOOKS: *Scenes of Clerical Life* (2 volumes, Edin-
burgh & London: Blackwood, 1858; 1 volume,
New York: Harper, 1858);
*Adam Bede* (3 volumes, Edinburgh & London:
Blackwood, 1859; 1 volume, New York:
Harper, 1859);
*The Mill on the Floss* (3 volumes, Edinburgh & Lon-
don: Blackwood, 1860; 1 volume, New York:
Harper, 1860);
*Silas Marner: The Weaver of Raveloe* (2 volumes,
Edinburgh & London: Blackwood, 1861; 1
volume, New York: Harper, 1861);
*Romola* (3 volumes, London: Smith, Elder, 1863; 1
volume, New York: Harper, 1863);
*Felix Holt, The Radical* (3 volumes, Edinburgh &
London: Blackwood, 1866; 1 volume, New
York: Harper, 1866);
*The Spanish Gypsy: A Poem* (Edinburgh & London:
Blackwood, 1868; Boston: Ticknor & Fields,
1868);

*George Eliot in 1860, drawn by Samuel Laurence*

Beginning of author bibliography

Fig. 44. The first page of the George Eliot entry from *Dictionary of Literary Biography* 21 (145).

compensate for these omissions. For biographies of deceased American
women writers, you should look in both the *DAB* and *NAW*.

If you need information on a writer who was alive when these
sources were published, you should turn to *Current Biography*. Issued
monthly and cumulated annually, it details the lives and achieve-
ments of famous persons in all professions around the world. Writers

are well represented. *Contemporary Authors* is a multivolume biographical encyclopedia specifically devoted to living writers. International in scope, it covers authors of works in various fields, including literature. Treatments are generally briefer than those in the *DLB*, the *DNB*, the *DAB*, *NAW*, and *Current Biography*. But *Contemporary Authors* does have the information about most writers on the current scene.

Those of you who prefer to work electronically may want to consult *Literary Index*, an online master index to a variety of literary reference series published by Gale including *Contemporary Authors* and *Dictionary of Literary Biography*. You will still need to consult the printed volumes for the actual information, but you can save yourself some time identifying the appropriate source by using this index first.

The single-volume biographical dictionaries of literary figures mentioned in the appendix are more restrictive in scope and coverage, affording each author a factual paragraph or two. But for basic data, they may be perfectly adequate.

Don't forget that you can find citations for biographies of individual authors in the online catalog. Most general encyclopedias, like *Encyclopedia Britannica* or the online version *Britannica Online*, have biographical information, too.

# In Quest of Quotations

In writing your term papers, you will undoubtedly use quotations from your primary source as documentation for your thesis. Most likely you will have noted the important passages in your copy of the novel, poem, play, or short story. But once in a while you will need to track down an elusive quotation to substantiate a point you wish to make. With so many primary texts becoming more and more available in electronic format, it will be increasingly easy to search the databases of these works by keyword. In the meantime, there are a couple of reference sources to assist you.

The first of these, the concordance, is an alphabetical index to all substantial words in an individual work or in a body of works. Concordances exist to different versions of the Bible and to the works of many major authors, such as Shakespeare. It is easy to appreciate the usefulness of this type of reference tool. If you were looking for the

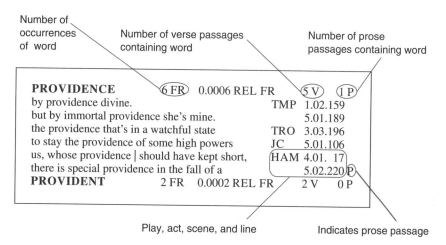

Fig. 45. An entry from Marvin Spevack, *The Harvard Concordance to Shakespeare* (1002); the listings identify passages by type (prose or verse) and specific location.

line in *Hamlet* "there is special providence in the fall of a sparrow," you could waste considerable time and energy thumbing randomly through your copy of the play, or you could consult *The Harvard Concordance to Shakespeare*. To track down the quotation in the concordance, you simply check the choices under one of the three keywords in the line: *fall*, *providence*, and *sparrow*. The word *fall* is so common that certainly too many quotations would appear under that term to make the line easy to find. In fact, *The Harvard Concordance to Shakespeare* has three columns of choices under *fall*. Under *providence*, however, there are only six quotations, the sixth being the one you want (fig. 45). It is in *Hamlet*, act 5, scene 2, line 220. The *P* following the citations in the concordance indicates a prose passage as opposed to one in verse. The age of computerization has brought an assortment of concordances to complement various works and authors. If your library has a concordance to the works of a specific author, the formal subject headings in the online catalog is under the author's name and the subdivision "—Concordance," as in "Shakespeare, William, 1564–1616—Concordance." You could also find this concordance by doing a keyword search in your online catalog, linking the words "Shakespeare" and "concordance" with "and."

You are not going to find a concordance for every author. If a quotation is fairly well known, it may appear in a dictionary of general quotations such as *The Oxford Dictionary of Quotations* or Bartlett's *Familiar Quotations*. The latter is also available on CD-ROM. Each of them has a keyword index to appropriate authors and sources. All these dictionaries, some of which are mentioned in the appendix, are selective, but all include some important quotations from literature. And, as you will see in the next section, one special English-language dictionary, the *Oxford English Dictionary*, can also serve as a dictionary of quotations in its electronic version.

## Facts from Dictionaries and Handbooks

When you need quick information, such as the definition of a word or the history of a literary concept, you head for an English-language dictionary or a literary handbook. You probably already own an abridged English-language dictionary or have access to one online. Good, inexpensive versions in electronic format or hard- or softcover have been available from Merriam-Webster, Random House, and Funk and Wagnalls for years. They usually suffice for everyday problems of spelling, pronunciation, and definition. In addition, the spell-check features of most word-processing software can assist with spelling. When a desk-size version fails to solve your problem, an unabridged dictionary, like *Webster's Third New International Dictionary of the English Language*, should be your next recourse. Whereas abridged dictionaries are limited to the most frequently used words, the unabridged strive to include all known words in the language with the possible exception of some slang or colloquial terms. Your college library most likely has an ample supply of both abridged and unabridged dictionaries. Many campuses have dictionaries available on their campus computer networks or in CD-ROM format.

As you study literature from earlier centuries, an etymological dictionary will prove invaluable. For every word ever known to exist in a particular language, this kind of dictionary supplies a history, the date of its first known recorded use, variant spellings and pronunciations, and distinctive usages. The multivolume *Oxford English Dictionary* (*OED*) is an excellent example. If you wanted to examine the possible meanings of the term *nunnery* in Hamlet's famous command to Ophelia, "Get thee to a nunnery!" (*Hamlet* 3.1.121), you would have to consult the *OED*. According to this dictionary, the term can mean either a residence for nuns or "a house of ill fame" (figs. 46a and b). Since the second usage was apparently introduced by Thomas Nashe in 1593, it would have been known during Shakespeare's time. The last volume of the *OED* provides full bibliographic information on Nashe's work as well as on other sources cited throughout the dictionary.

---

**nunnery** ('nʌnərɪ). Forms: *a.* 3–7 **nonnerie,** 3–5 **-erye,** 4, 6 **nonery,** 6 **noonery.** *β.* 4, 7 **nunnerie,** 5 **nvnnerye,** 6– **nunnery** (7 **nunery**). [Prob. ad. AF. \**nonnerie*, f. *nonne* NUN *sb.*¹: see -ERY. Cf. F. *nonnerie* (Littré).]

**1.** A place of residence for a body or community of nuns; a building in which nuns live under religious rule and discipline; a convent.

*a.* *c* **1275** LAY. 15642 Nou was Merlyn his moder . . in one nonnerie munechene ihoded. *c* **1290** *S. Eng. Leg.* I. 91/148 And al þis compaygnie I-burede weren in Coloyne, in one Nonnerie. *c* **1330** R. BRUNNE *Chron. Wace* (Rolls) 14225 Scheo ȝald hure til þat nonnerye, & tok þe veil for hure folye. *c* **1386** CHAUCER *Reeve's T.* 48 For hir kynreed and hir nortelrye, That sche had lerned in a nonnerye. *c* **1425** *Hampole's Psalter* Metr. Pref. 28 par it lyȝt in cheyn bondes in þe same nonery. **1470–85** MALORY *Arthur* XXI. ix. 854 Atte last he cam to a nonnerye. **1523** LD. BERNERS *Froiss.* I. CXXV. 151 The kyng of Englande was at Poissoy, and lay in the nonery there. *c* **1612** *Women Saints* 55 Her sister St. Etheldred . . founder of that Nonnerie.

*β.* *c* **1305** *Land Cokayne* 147 An oþer abbei is þerbi For soth a gret fair nunnerie. **1483** *Cath. Angl.* 257/1 A Nvnnerye, *cenobium*. **1571** A. JENKINSON *Voy. & Trav.* (Hakl. Soc.) I. 137 Not farre from the said Castle was a Nunnery of sumptuous building. **1602** SHAKS. *Ham.* III. i. 122 Get thee to a Nunnerie. *Ibid.* 132 Goe thy wayes to a Nunnery. **1648** GAGE *West Ind.* 58 This man alone built a Nunery of Franciscan Nuns. *a* **1699** LADY HALKETT *Autobiog.* (Camden) 15 That there was a nunery in Holland for those of the Protestant relligion. **1707** LADY M. W. MONTAGU *Lett.* II. xlvii. 43 Her relations . . would certainly confine her to a nunnery for the rest of her days. **1756–7** tr. *Keysler's Trav.* (1760) II. 229 There are boards placed before most of the windows, like those in a great many nunneries. **1841** ELPHINSTONE *Hist. Ind.* I. 201 Nunneries for women seem also, at one time, to have been general. **1886** *Pall Mall G.* 17 July 5/2 To the south-east we may see the ruins of Sopwell nunnery.

*fig.* **1634** HABINGTON *Castara* I. (Arb.) 18 Yee blushing Virgins [*sc.* roses] happie are In the chaste Nunn'ry of her brests. **1652** CRASHAW *Elegy Mr. Stanninow*, Whose nest Was in the modest Nunnery of his brest.

*attrib.* **1859** TENNYSON *Guinev.* 225 O little maid, shut in by nunnery walls. **1884** J. HALL *Christian Home* 113 When no safety could be hoped for California girls but in nunnery schools.

---

Fig. 46a. A portion of the entry for *nunnery* in *The Oxford English Dictionary*, 2nd ed.

**b.** *transf.* A house of ill fame.
**1593** NASHE *Christ's T.* 79 b, [To] some one Gentleman generally acquainted, they giue . . free priuiledge thence-forward in theyr Nunnery, to procure them frequentance. **1617** FLETCHER *Mad Lover* IV. ii, Theres an old Nunnerie at hand. What's that? A bawdy-house. **17** . . (*title-p.*), The Complete London Spy, or Disclosures of the Transactions in and around London and Westminster Coffee houses, Nunneries, Night Houses, Taverns, Bagnios, etc.

Fig. 46b. A portion of the entry for *nunnery* in *The Oxford English Dictionary*, 2nd ed.

Since 1987, all twelve volumes of the *OED* have been available on CD-ROM. Similarly, some libraries have an electronic version of this work available on their campus networks. Unlike the printed version, which limits your access solely to looking up a specific work, the electronic versions of the *OED* offer more search paths than just the lemma (the headword for each entry). You can seek out an etymology, a definition, a part of speech, a subject category, a place-name, or a quotation. To find a quotation, you can ask the computer to search for the quotation itself or for its date, author, or source. In other words, the electronic version of the *OED* is not just the standard etymological dictionary of the English language but also a powerful dictionary of quotations—another example of the way in which automation can make an important reference work even more useful.

For general information on an author or a literary period, for the identification of characters, or for the definitions of literary terms, a handbook is your best tool. *The Oxford Companion to English Literature*, *The Oxford Companion to American Literature*, and *The Oxford Companion to Women's Writing in the United States* are excellent, easy-to-use, single-volume handbooks. Each has basic biographical information about authors, brief plot summaries of major works, short definitions of literary terms and concepts, and general outlines of literary movements. For example, if you needed some background information on the epistolary novel in the context of American women authors, *The Oxford Companion to Women's Writing in the United States* offers an excellent brief essay (fig. 47). These three handbooks

**EPISTOLARY NOVEL.** Although American women have produced few epistolary novels, the literary significance of those that exist is much greater than simple numbers would suggest. Since an epistolary novel is composed of an exchange of *letters, a correspondence among its characters, it does not contain the explicit guiding, framing, and potentially dominating presence of a narrative persona. The epistolary novel offers readers direct and potentially equal access to the voices of its characters. For this reason, the epistolary novel has served as a vehicle for authors who wish to present voices marginal to the dominant cultural experience—voices traditionally muted or submerged. From Hannah Webster *Foster's *The Coquette* (1797), to Alice *Walker's *The Color Purple* (1982), Ana *Castillo's *The Mixquiahuala Letters* (1986), and Lee *Smith's *Fair and Tender Ladies* (1988), the epistolary novel has offered women writers a way to privilege voices that might not otherwise be heard.

The epistolary novel emerged in eighteenth-century Europe from the tradition of genteel

Fig. 47. A portion of the entry for *epistolary novel* in *The Oxford Companion to Women's Writings in the United States* (275).

each focus on a nationality and gender; others, like the *New Princeton Encyclopedia of Poetry and Poetics*, are organized around specific genres. It is a good idea to consult a handbook whenever you do not clearly understand some term. Several other literary handbooks and English-language dictionaries are noted in the appendix.

## Guidelines on Form

As you prepare the final draft of your term paper, you will undoubtedly want to make sure that your work, especially its documentation and bibliography, is presented in an acceptable form. The *MLA Handbook for Writers of Research Papers* describes the conventions for written literary research that are approved by scholars and college professors. It briefly discusses the process of selecting and researching a topic as well as the mechanics of writing critical prose. There are over a hundred examples of reference notes and bibliographic entries intended to illustrate the citation of every conceivable kind of source that you might use, including those in electronic format. Sample pages of a research paper are given, too, to help you set up your paper according to the recommended format. A detailed index makes this handbook particularly easy to use. The most recent edition of the *MLA Handbook*, the fifth, is most likely available at your library, but if you plan to write many literary research papers, you will want to obtain your own copy.

Those of you who are especially computer literate will be pleased to learn that software has been developed that will convert the bibliographic information that you download from an electronic index or bibliography, such as the *MLA Bibliography*, into the proper citation format according to the *MLA Handbook*. Such programs as *EndNote* and *ProCite* allow you to convert your references to the proper format automatically at your microcomputer workstation. These management software products are especially helpful when managing extensive files of bibliographic information on your desktop workstation. For more information on these programs, see the appendix.

CHAPTER SIX

# Using Primary Sources

Moreover, no one writes in a vacuum. Whatever private in-
fluences are involved, authors, whether conformists or
rebels, are the products of time and place, their mental set
fatefully determined by the social and cultural
environment. To understand a book, we must also understand the manifold socially derived attitudes—the morality,
the myths, the assumptions, the biases—that it reflects or
embraces.
—Richard D. Altick and John J. Fenstermaker,
*The Art of Literary Research*

For much of the work you undertake as a student of English or
American literature, finding secondary books and articles will be sufficient for your research. But some classes may require you to look
into primary sources, those documents written during the time period
that you are studying, as a way of putting a piece of literature or a
theme in literature in context.

Primary sources in literature consist of the work of literature itself as well as the author's diaries, journals, and autobiography. What
a writer reveals in an autobiography or diary may help you understand the themes of a particular novel, poem, or short story. Beyond
these more obvious resources lie a wealth of additional primary
sources reflecting the time during which the author lived. In times
past, these sources may have been available only to a few scholars

who could travel to the great libraries in England or the United States to research the collections. Through the wonders of microform and digital reproduction, many important collections can be perused at libraries throughout the country and, in some cases, on your computer. The Library of Congress and many universities are offering selective primary texts in Web-based format over the Internet.

What types of primary sources might help you to place a work or a theme in literature in its cultural and social context? Examples include newspaper and periodical articles published during the time period; the diaries, journals, and correspondence of people living during that time; and Congressional and Parliamentary debates. Identifying appropriate primary sources is a challenge and requires a variety of research techniques. A few of these are illustrated through the following example.

Reading Charles Dickens's novel *Oliver Twist*, you wonder about the lives and treatment of city children in Britain during the nineteenth century. Checking your library catalog using the keywords "children" and "England" and "history" and "nineteenth century," you find a book by Eric Hopkins called *Childhood Transformed: Working-Class Children in Nineteenth-Century England*. Another book found in this search is Pamela Horn's *The Victorian Town Child*, which specifically addresses the social conditions of city children. In addition to providing contextual information, these secondary sources include bibliographies that identify the primary sources consulted by the authors.

One key to finding primary sources through the catalog is to combine major subject headings with the word *sources*, which will find collections of primary sources. An example of a book found in the University of Washington Libraries under the subject heading "Children—Great Britain—History—Sources" is Irina Strickland's *The Voices of Children, 1700–1914*. (figs. 48a and b). Arranged chronologically, this book contains excerpts of original writings that touch on all aspects of the lives of children, including employment and living conditions. Not all libraries use the word *sources*, and it is possible to find primary sources either in collections or as individual publications through standard subject searching. To find the letters of an individual, combine the word *correspondence* with the name. In the University of Washington Libraries catalog, a search using the subject

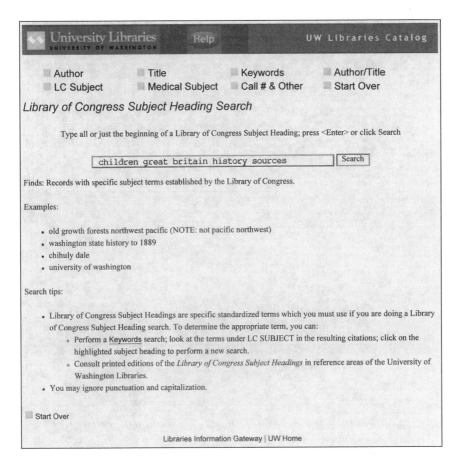

Fig. 48a. Library of Congress subject heading search using the keywords *children*, *great britain*, *history*, and *sources* from the University of Washington online catalog.

heading "Dickens, Charles, 1812–1870—Correspondence" lists such books as *Selected Letters of Charles Dickens*, edited and arranged by David Pariossien. A collection of Dickens's letters may provide further information about his views on the treatment of children.

Looking at the bibliography in Hopkins's *Childhood Transformed* indicates that he used a number of government publications of the time in writing his book. In addition to checking the documents he cites, you could consult British parliamentary debates and sessional papers for further information on the treatment of children during the

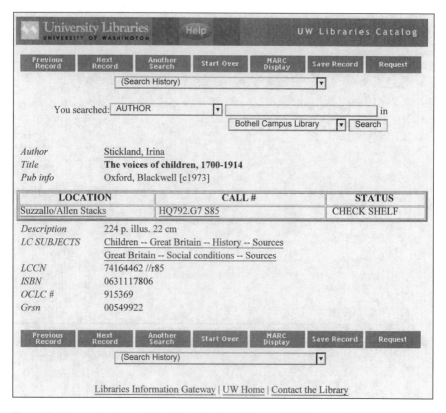

Fig. 48b. Entry for Irina Strickland's *The Voices of Children, 1700–1914*, retrieved from the keyword subject heading search using the University of Washington online catalog.

nineteenth century. Check your library's catalog by keyword or author to find such references as *Parliamentary Debates* (generally cited as *Hansard's Parliamentary Debates*) and *Subject Catalogue of the House of Commons Parliamentary Papers, 1801–1900*. Because the indexes to British official publications changed names several times during the course of the century, ask your reference librarian to assist you in finding the years you need.

Primary information can also be found by using guides and indexes to the periodicals and newspapers of the day. *Poole's Index to Periodical Literature, 1802–1907* is an index by subject to articles published in some of the leading magazines of the time and can be consulted for topics related to the United Kingdom and the United States.

*The Wellesley Index to Victorian Periodicals, 1824–1900* is organized by the title of the periodical and lists the contents for each issue. There is no subject index in the print version, but you can quickly scan the listings for the years in which you are interested. For example, the contents for the September 1836 issue include an article called "Glances at Life in City and Suburb," which would provide some background on general life around the time that Dickens wrote *Oliver Twist* (fig. 49). There is now a CD-ROM version of *Wellesley* that can be searched by keywords in titles. Finally, *Palmer's Index to the* Times *(London), 1790–1905*, available in electronic or paper form, is a subject listing of articles published in the newspaper for the period of time indicated. Your library may have the *Times* on microfilm. Some publishers have also microfilmed collections of periodicals and newspapers from the nineteenth and other centuries. Check with your reference librarian to see what might be available in your library.

So far we have focused on primary sources related to Great Britain in the nineteenth century. This same research process can be used for other periods and for the United States. If you were interested in finding primary sources related to issues raised in Upton Sinclair's *The Jungle*, published in 1906, you would want to check United States congressional publications such as hearings and laws. To find out what might be written on the meatpacking industry and on the condition of factories, consult the *New York Times Index* and the *Reader's Guide to Periodical Literature*.

Primary sources bring the period you are studying alive and allow you to develop your own interpretation in relation to the work or works you are reading rather than rely completely on secondary material. Identifying and tracking down primary sources can be a challenge. Doubtless this task will be facilitated over time by the digitization of major primary documents and finding aids and their accessibility through the Web. It is important to remember, however, that sometimes pieces of text are pulled out of context and that you may still need to use printed resources to find a source in its entirety.

> **510** *Glances at Life in City and Suburb,*
> 223–229. **J. G. Lockhart.** Murray.

Fig. 49. Entry 510 from *The Wellesley Index to Victorian Periodicals, 1824–1900* (718).

# CHAPTER SEVEN

# Pulling It All Together

As noted in earlier chapters, there is a growing trend toward linking together the different kinds of information found in a variety of electronic databases, making it easier for researchers to locate all the information they need. For example, you may want factual, biographical information on an author, a list of his or her works, a copy of some of these works, and a list of the critical articles pertaining to one of the works. To acquire this information by using many of the sources described earlier in this book, you would need to check each database or printed work separately. Increasingly, the database producers are providing links between their many electronic products and other databases. As students of literature become more and more computer literate, there is a growing expectation of links among these different literary reference sources.

*Literature Online* (*LION*) is one such source. This database is actually a conglomerate of over a dozen separate literary collections currently offered on microfilm or electronically by Chadwyck-Healey. *LION Complete* conveniently brings together the information found in all these databases. *LION Poetry* is limited to their poetry databases. Both packages include access to the *King James Bible*, *Merriam Webster's Dictionary*, the *Annual Bibliography of English Language and Literature*, and *Literary Journals Index Full Text* (*LIFT*). As appropriate, there are links to Gale's *Literature Resource Center* (ch. 3) and to Web resources on the Internet.

*LION* allows you to find background information on English and American authors, lists of their works, the texts of many of these primary works, lists of secondary critical studies pertaining to these works, and any relevant Web sites. In other words, it brings together sources that have historically been published in separate reference books. Chadwyck-Healey continues to add to the *LION* database. At the time this chapter was written, the primary texts of some nineteenth-century fiction, early American fiction, and American drama were being added to *LION Complete*.

Let's look at a typical search using *LION Complete*. The first screen gives you a very brief description of the scope of the database, a listing of the search options, and an opportunity to learn more about *Literature Online*. You can find authors; find works by title; browse a list of authors (especially helpful if you are not sure of the author's name); search a specific text by keyword, literary period, date, or author; search secondary sources from *Annual Bibliography of English Language and Literature* and *Literary Journals Index Full Text*; and search additional literary databases (fig. 50).

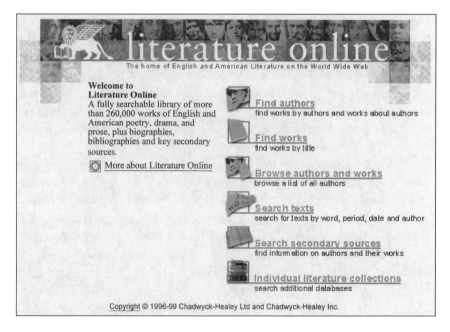

Fig. 50. Welcome screen on *Literature Online*.

Let's assume you want information on Anne Killigrew, a seventeenth-century poet. You might start with some basic biographical information. Although it is possible to limit an author search by dates, the author's gender, or literary period, a simple search of "Anne Killigrew," without additional qualifiers, proves sufficient for this author (fig. 51). (If you were searching for an author with a more common name, you might find that using qualifiers is especially helpful.) You are then asked whether you want Anne Killigrew's biography, works by her, or works about her (fig. 52). In this particular example, the biographical information is limited to dates of birth and death, her

# Find authors

Who Wrote...?

Submit Search

**Author Name**  killigrew, anne     Browse

**Living in the year(s)**  From 600 to 1999

**Gender**  Female or male authors ▼

**Literary Period**  All Literary Periods
Anglo-Saxon Poetry 600-1100
Medieval Drama 1280-1500

**Who Wrote...?**

Enter the whole title of the work or keywords from the title into the box below and click **Find**.

Find

Copyright © 1996-99 Chadwyck-Healey Ltd and Chadwyck-Healey Inc.

Fig. 51. Author search of Anne Killigrew on *Literature Online*.

# Summary of results (Authors)

Your search **Author Name(s): killigrew, anne** found **1 author(s)**.

1.  **Killigrew, Anne, 1660-1685**     Biography     Works By     Works About

Copyright © 1996-99 Chadwyck-Healey Ltd and Chadwyck-Healey Inc.

Fig. 52. Results of search for author Anne Killigrew on *Literature Online*.

## Anne Killigrew (1660-1685)

Works By Killigrew | Works About Killigrew

**Dates of Birth/Death:** 1660-1685
**Gender:** Female
**Literary Movements/Periods:** Restoration 1660-1700

Read more about Killigrew at The Gale Group's Literature Resource Center

Fig. 53. Biographical data on Anne Killigrew from *Literature Online.*

## Eve Merriam (1916-1992)

Works By Merriam | Works About Merriam

**Dates of Birth/Death:** 1916-1992
**Gender:** Female
**Literary Movements/Periods:** Twentieth-Century 1900-1999

**Biography**

Eve Merriam, whose name was originally Eva Moskovitz, was born in 1916 in Philadelphia, Pennsylvania. She attended the University of Pennsylvania (AB, 1937) and did graduate work at Columbia University and the University of Wisconsin. Her early work was as a radio writer in New York City (1939-1946). During this period she also contributed features and occasional light verse to a number of magazines. After the success of her first book of poetry,*Family Circle* (1946), she became a freelance writer. She also taught creative writing at the City College of New York (1965-1969).

Merriam is known mainly for her many volumes of verse for juvenile readers, but she was also a prolific playwright and writer of poetry with more mature themes. Her lyrical, rhyming verse addressed issues that ranged from the observational and incidental to issues of national importance. She addressed her readers, whether in the nursery or grown up, with the same respect and wry humor. One of her favorite themes in prose and poetry was to write about the creative process. She was a prolific writer, publishing more than one hundred plays and volumes of poetry.

Merriam's poetry for adults include *Family Circle* (1946), *Tomorrow Morning* (1953), *Montgomery, Alabama, Money, Mississippi, and Other Places* (1956), *The Double Bed from the Feminine Side* (1958), *The Trouble with Love* (1960), *The Inner City Mother Goose* (1969), *The Nixon Poems* (1970) and *A Husband's Notes About Her* (1976). She was the winner of numerous awards and honors for her works of juvenile poetry and fiction and for her plays. For her adult poetry, she was awarded the Yale Younger Poets Prize (1946).

Fig. 54. Biographical information on Eve Merriam from *Literature Online.*

gender, and literary period (fig. 53). Notice the reference to Gale's *Literature Resource Center.* For many authors, there is also a substantial biographical-critical essay on the author. The entry for Eve Merriam is a good example of a more detailed biographical account (fig. 54). For some authors, a portrait photograph is also provided.

If you click on "Works by Killigrew," just above her dates of birth and death on the biography screen, you find a bibliography of poems by Anne Killigrew (fig. 55). There are thirty-one poems, no prose works, no drama, and five "WWW texts" sites. If you click on any of the poem titles, you are taken to the text of that poem, as long as it is part of the database. Not all bibliographic citations for all authors will be linked to full text. If you select poem 2, "A Farewel to Worldly Joys,"

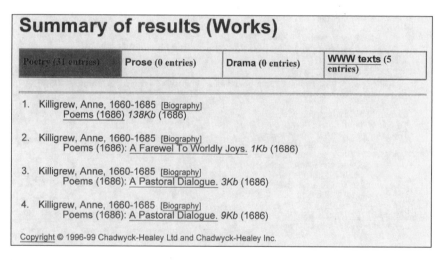

Fig. 55. Portion of the list of works by Anne Killigrew from *Literature Online.*

you can see the poem's full text (fig. 56). You can also find a listing of five pertinent Web sites by clicking on the "WWW texts" bar (fig. 57).

If you need a list of secondary sources (i.e., books or articles of literary criticism on Anne Killigrew's poetry), back up to her biography screen and click on "works about Killigrew." You could also return to the original menu screen, select "search secondary sources," and then type in the author's name. But in this case it would be simpler to back up only as far as the biography screen. Four items are listed, all taken from the *Annual Bibliography of English Language and Literature (ABELL)* (fig. 58). The article by Robert Daly can be found in *Texas*

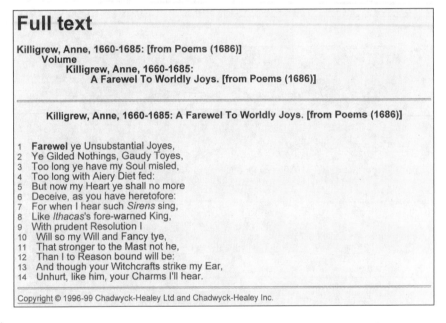

Fig. 56. The poem "A Farewel to Worldly Joys," by Anne Killigrew, from *Literature Online.*

## Summary of results (Works)

| Poetry (31 entries) | Prose (0 entries) | Drama (0 entries) | WWW texts (5 entries) |
|---|---|---|---|

1. Killigrew, Anne, 1660-1685 [Biography]
   First EPIGRAM.Vpon being Contented with a Little (Representative Poetry, University of Toronto Press) *1Kb*

2. Killigrew, Anne, 1660-1685 [Biography]
   On Death (Representative Poetry, University of Toronto Press) *2Kb*

3. Killigrew, Anne, 1660-1685 [Biography]
   SELECTED POETRY OF ANNE KILLIGREW (Representative Poetry, University of Toronto Press) *4Kb*

4. Killigrew, Anne, 1660-1685 [Biography]
   The Discontent (Representative Poetry, University of Toronto Press) *10Kb*

5. Killigrew, Anne, 1660-1685 [Biography]
   The Miseries of Man (Representative Poetry, University of Toronto Press) *13Kb*

Copyright © 1996-99 Chadwyck-Healey Ltd and Chadwyck-Healey Inc.

Fig. 57. Listing of World Wide Web sites pertaining to Anne Killigrew from *Literature Online*.

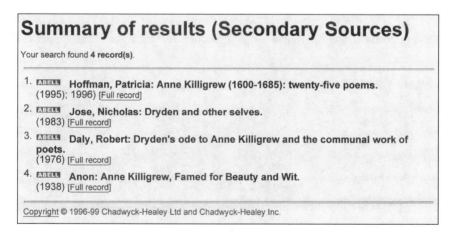

## Summary of results (Secondary Sources)

Your search found **4 record(s)**.

1. **[ABELL]** **Hoffman, Patricia: Anne Killigrew (1600-1685): twenty-five poems.**
   (1995); 1996) [Full record]

2. **[ABELL]** **Jose, Nicholas: Dryden and other selves.**
   (1983) [Full record]

3. **[ABELL]** **Daly, Robert: Dryden's ode to Anne Killigrew and the communal work of poets.**
   (1976) [Full record]

4. **[ABELL]** **Anon: Anne Killigrew, Famed for Beauty and Wit.**
   (1938) [Full record]

Copyright © 1996-99 Chadwyck-Healey Ltd and Chadwyck-Healey Inc.

Fig. 58. Listing of literary criticism on the works of Anne Killigrew from *Literature Online*.

*Studies in Literature and Language: A Journal of the Humanities* (fig. 59). You currently cannot link directly to the text of this article since *ABELL*, from which this entry was derived, does not include full text. Had the entry been taken from *Literary Journal Index Full Text* (*LIFT*), there might have been full text of the article. At this time *Literary Journal Index Full Text*, while indexing around two hundred journals, only includes full text for about thirty of these journals. We would not be surprised to see the number of full-text articles in *LION* continue to increase.

It is possible to refine your search for secondary sources by keyword subject, title, journal, author or reviewer, and year of publication. For journals published after 1998, you can also limit your search to a specified list of literary periods, literary movements, types of documents, and literary genres (fig. 60). For a search on an author like Killigrew, with a limited range of poems and literary criticism, this would not be necessary. But for a search on a more prolific writer, the ability to refine your search for secondary sources could prove useful. You can reach this search screen by selecting "search secondary sources" on the first menu screen of *LION* (fig. 50)

The online instructions for searching *LION*, accessible through the "help" option, are clearly written and easy to follow. Do not hesitate to consult the online instructions for any database when using it

## Full record

⟨⟨  First   ⟨ Previous Record      Next Record ⟩   Last  ⟩⟩

| | | |
|---|---|---|
| | **ABELL** | |
| 3. | **Author:** | Daly, Robert. |
| | **Title:** | **Dryden's ode to Anne Killigrew and the communal work of poets.** |
| | **Publication Details:** | Texas Studies in Literature and Language: a journal of the humanities (Univ. of Texas, Austin) (18) 184-97. |
| | **Publication Year:** | 1976 |
| | **Subject:** | •English Literature: Seventeenth Century: Authors: Dryden, John •English Literature: Seventeenth Century: Authors: Killigrew, Anne |
| | **ABELL ref:** | 1976:5371; 1976:5557 |

Copyright © 1996-99 Chadwyck-Healey Ltd and Chadwyck-Healey Inc.

Fig. 59. Entry for Robert Daly's essay in *Texas Studies in Literature* from *Literature Online.*

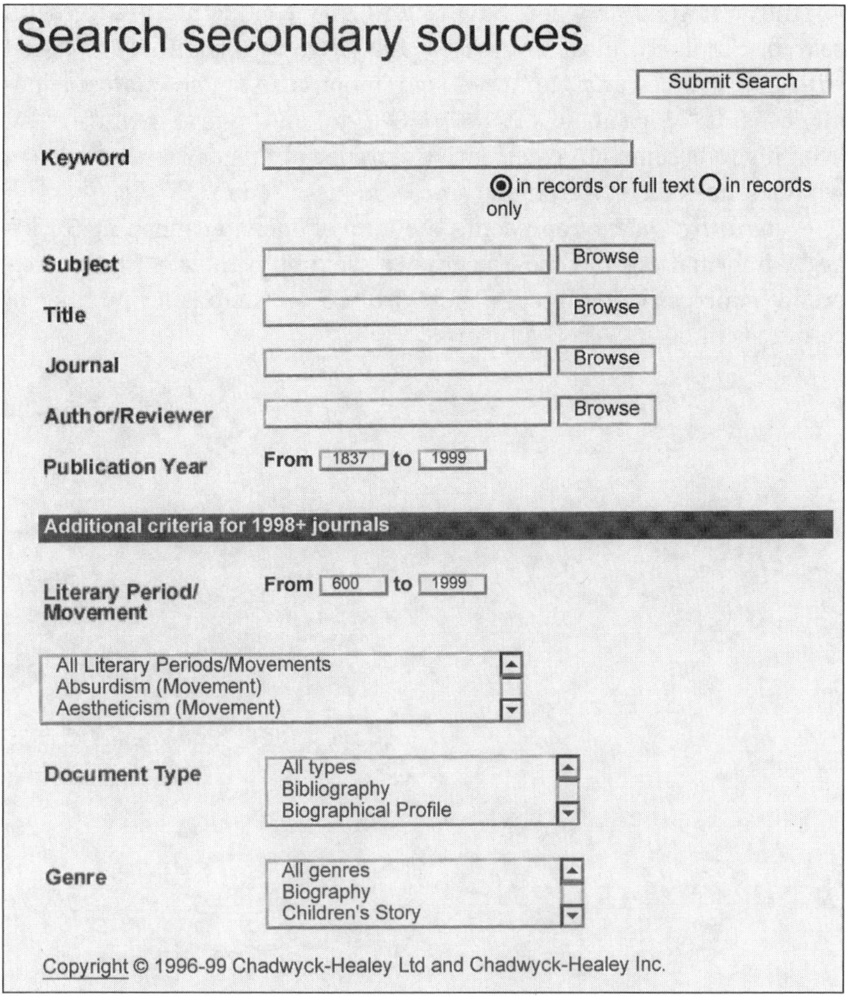

# Search secondary sources

| Submit Search |

**Keyword**

⦿ in records or full text ◯ in records only

**Subject** [ Browse ]

**Title** [ Browse ]

**Journal** [ Browse ]

**Author/Reviewer** [ Browse ]

**Publication Year** From [ 1837 ] to [ 1999 ]

**Additional criteria for 1998+ journals**

**Literary Period/ Movement** From [ 600 ] to [ 1999 ]

All Literary Periods/Movements
Absurdism (Movement)
Aestheticism (Movement)

**Document Type**

All types
Bibliography
Biographical Profile

**Genre**

All genres
Biography
Children's Story

Copyright © 1996-99 Chadwyck-Healey Ltd and Chadwyck-Healey Inc.

Fig. 60. "Search secondary sources" screen from *Literature Online.*

for the first time or when having difficulty conducting a successful search. Similarly, most databases like *LION* are routinely updated with new sources and enhanced search options. You should occasionally consult "More about *Literature Online*" on the first menu screen, even if you become an experienced searcher of this database, to learn what changes have been made since you last used *LION*.

*Literature Online* represents the kind of one-stop shopping for literary information that most users are seeking in their electronic reference sources. Undoubtedly there will be an increasing number of resources like *LION* in the future.

CHAPTER EIGHT

# Guides to Research in Literature

Throughout this guide we have concentrated on literary research, emphasizing only about forty-five reference sources. Of course, many other indexes, bibliographies, dictionaries, handbooks, and related tools may become helpful as you develop your knowledge and skills in the study of English and American literature. These works are cited in literary guides that provide broader coverage than is appropriate here.

The most extensive current guide to research tools in British, American, and other English-language literatures is James L. Harner's *Literary Research Guide*. Annotations are provided for most entries, accurately describing the reference sources and evaluating their overall quality and usefulness. If you have extensive research projects or plan to attend graduate school, you should, or rather must, become familiar with this excellent guide.

No discussion of research guides would be complete without some mention of Robert Balay's *Guide to Reference Books*. Listing all major reference books in all disciplines, this is the reference librarian's right hand. It is without a doubt the most comprehensive bibliography of reference sources currently available. Most entries are annotated. Its organization, first by discipline and then by type of reference tool, makes it especially easy to use. Previous editions of this book were written by Eugene Sheehy, and many experienced librarians may still refer to it as Sheehy.

These two guides to literature, along with two others, are listed in the appendix.

# Selective Bibliography of Reference Sources for English and American Literature

In the following bibliography of reference tools, the section headings match the chapters or subdivisions that treat the types of sources listed. The asterisks designate entries mentioned in the text.

## 1. Conducting Research in an Electronic Environment

Grassian, Esther. "Thinking Critically about World Wide Web Resources." 1997. Regents of the Univ. of California. <http://www.library.ucla .edu/libraries/college/instruct/web/critical.htm>.
Written by a veteran librarian at UCLA's College Library, this concise list identifies a number of factors to consider when looking at Web sites. Her "Thinking Critically about Discipline-Based World Wide Web Resources" (http://www.library.ucla.edu/libraries/college/instruct/web/discp.htm) is also useful.

*Harner, James L. *Literary Research Guide: An Annotated Listing of*

*Reference Sources in Literary Studies.* 3rd ed. New York: MLA, 1998.

This standard guide to sources in literature features a short chapter on Internet resources. Chapter 8 provides a more detailed description of this book.

Joseph, Nancy L. *Research Writing Using Traditional and Electronic Sources.* Upper Saddle River: Prentice, 1999.

This practical and readable book guides students through the entire research process. The sections on evaluating print and online sources are excellent and illustrated with examples. A study companion for the book is available on the Web (http://cw.prenhall.com/bookbind/public_html/pubbooks/joseph/).

*\*JSTOR.* 2000. JSTOR. <http://www.jstor.org>.

*JSTOR* offers the noncurrent issues of major scholarly journals in many disciplines. If your library subscribes to *JSTOR*, you can search the database for articles by subject. Some of the literature journals are *African-American Review* (1967–95), *American Literature* (1929–1993), *ELH* (1934–94), and *Shakespeare Quarterly* (1950–93).

*\*Literary Resources on the Net.* Dec. 1999. <http://andromeda.rutgers.edu/~jlynch/Lit/>.

Maintained by Jack Lynch, an assistant professor of English at Rutgers University, Newark, this page lists Web sites devoted to English and American literature.

*\*Project Muse.* Johns Hopkins UP. < http://muse.jhu.edu>.

*Project Muse* provides online subscription access to the full texts of forty of Johns Hopkins University Press's periodical titles. A few of the literature titles are *Eighteenth Century Studies*, *Modern Fiction Studies*, *New Literary History*, and the *Yale Journal of Criticism*.

Rodrigues, Dawn. *The Research Paper and the World Wide Web.* 2nd ed. Upper Saddle River: Prentice, 2000.

The author provides detailed information on using the World Wide Web for research and covers everything from navigation to using e-mail and newsgroups as research tools. Especially helpful is her chapter "Library and Web Resources," which provides clear examples of what can be found at no cost on the Web and what is proprietary information available only by subscription. Another chapter discusses finding resources in the disciplines. A section on evaluating resources has been added to this new edition. Chapter overviews, updates, supplemental information, and links to all the Web sites mentioned can be found on the book's home page (http://www.prenhall.com/rodrigues).

*Voice of the Shuttle: Web Page for Humanities Research. Apr. 2000.*
    <http://vos.ucsb.edu/>.
Created by Alan Liu, professor of English at the University of California,
Santa Barbara, this page is devoted to Web sites in the humanities, in-
cluding literature, literary theory, and history.

# 2. Searching for Books

*Library of Congress Subject Headings.* 21st ed. Washington: Lib. of
    Congress, 1998.
These volumes list the terms and phrases used as formal subject headings in online catalogs.

# 3. Searching for Articles

*Annual Bibliography of English Language and Literature.* Cambridge:
    Mod. Humanities Research Assn., 1921– .
This bibliography of English and American literature indexes books,
pamphlets, dissertations, and periodical articles. References to book reviews are placed alongside citations for books. The language section is
arranged by subject, the literature section by literary period. The index
for literary authors, subjects, and critical authors makes this bibliography particularly easy to use. Entries from this bibliography are also represented in *Literature Online.*

*Annual Bibliography for English Studies.* CD-ROM. Lisse, Neth.: Swets
    and Zeitlinger, 1997– .

*Annual Bibliography for English Studies.* Online. Lisse, Neth.: Swets and
    Zeitlinger, 1999– .
Unlike the *MLA Bibliography,* this bibliography does not attempt to provide comprehensive coverage of the secondary material in English and
American literature. Instead it aims to offer bibliographic references to
the best studies from the last two centuries, based on the recommenda-
tions of about 450 subject specialists from all over the world. Coverage includes books, articles, and videos. Entries are annotated. The CD-ROM is
updated every six months.

*Contemporary Literary Criticism.* Detroit: Gale, 1973– .
This large, ongoing publication excerpts critiques, published primarily
within the past twenty-five years, of literary works by writers who are

living or who have died since 1 January 1960. Arrangement is by author, but there is a separate title index. A full citation follows each excerpt. An online version, *Contemporary Literary Criticism Select*, provides subject-term searching capability and an index that covers every volume in the series. The initial release of *Contemporary Literary Criticism Select* includes 100 authors, half derived from volumes 95–99. The other half represent major retrospective authors from the earlier volumes. Gale also publishes a variety of sources that offer excerpts of literary criticism, including *Black Literature Criticism*, *Drama Criticism*, *Nineteenth Century Literary Criticism*, *Poetry Criticism*, *Short Story Criticism*, and *Twentieth Century Criticism*.

*\*Expanded Academic ASAP*. Online. Farmington Hills: Gale, 1984– .
This online index provides citations to articles and book reviews published in several thousand general-interest and scholarly periodicals in the humanities, social sciences, and sciences. Almost all periodicals indexed in *Humanities Index* are also indexed in *Expanded Academic ASAP*. This index is an excellent place to begin a search for literary criticism or for articles pertaining to a theme in literature.

*\*Humanities Index*. New York: Wilson, 1975– .
Entitled *International Index to Periodicals* from 1920 to 1955 and *Social Sciences and Humanities Index* from 1965 to 1974, this index furnishes easy access to articles in nearly 300 periodicals for the humanities. The print version features author and subject indexing, making it an especially good source for interdisciplinary topics. A compilation of book reviews concludes each issue. Online versions, beginning in 1984, are available through OCLC's *FirstSearch*. You can also subscribe to the CD-ROM version, or the magnetic tape version can be loaded on the campus network.

*\*Literary Resource Center*. Online. Farmington Hills: Gale, 1998– .
This database conveniently combines three literary databases, also from Gale, for biographical information, bibliographic listings of authors' works, and critical analyses of more than 90,000 novelists, poets, essayists, journalists, and other writers. Search results may include links to Web sites and other special resources.

*\*MLA International Bibliography of Books and Articles on the Modern Languages and Literatures*. New York: MLA, 1922– .
From 1922 through 1955, this source listed only studies written by Americans. In 1956, it began international coverage by including writers from other countries. Since 1969, the scope has been further expanded to include books, dissertations, essays in Festschriften, and articles in over 2,000 international periodicals. The arrangement is first by author's na-

tionality or language, then by literary period, and then alphabetically by author. Publication is delayed by a year. Subject indexing was introduced with the 1981 volume. There is also a CD-ROM version from SilverPlatter covering 1963 to the present. OCLC *FirstSearch*, Ovid, and SilverPlatter also offer electronic access to the *MLA Bibliography* from 1963. The electronic versions offer a much broader range of searching options.

*ProQuest 3.0.* Online. Ann Arbor: Bell and Howell Information and Learning, 1999– .

This online index provides access to over 8,000 periodicals. Many of the periodicals provide full-text or full-image articles. The index is accessible over the Internet and has a variety of searching capabilities for the novice and experienced searcher.

# 4. Finding Book Reviews

*Annual Bibliography of English Language and Literature.* Cambridge: Mod. Humanities Research Assn., 1921– .

This bibliography of English and American literature, discussed in chapter 3, indexes books, pamphlets, dissertations, and periodical articles. References to book reviews are placed alongside citations for books. The index for literary authors, subjects, and critical authors makes this bibliography particularly easy to use. Entries from this bibliography are also represented in *Literature Online*.

*Book Review Digest.* New York: Wilson, 1905– .

To be included in this index, a work of nonfiction must have been reviewed at least twice; a work of fiction three times. Before the 1991 volume, works of fiction had to be reviewed at least four times. The entries, arranged by author, often give brief excerpts from the reviews, both favorable and unfavorable. A word count indicates the length of each review. Citations from 1983 to the present are accessible in electronic format on CD-ROM, through *WilsonWeb,* and through OCLC's *FirstSearch*.

*Book Review Index.* Detroit: Gale, 1965–69, 1972– .

More comprehensive than *Book Review Digest,* this source lists all book reviews, of both fiction and nonfiction, appearing in over 600 selected periodicals. But it dates back only to 1965 and provides no excerpts of reviews. Beginning with the 1992 volume, the index includes approximate word counts. *Dialog* offers online access to this index from 1969 to the present. It is also available on CD-ROM or on magnetic tape accessible over computer networks at subscribing campuses.

*Expanded Academic ASAP*. Farmington Hills: Gale, 1980– .
See description above under chapter 3.

*Index to Book Reviews in the Humanities*. Williamston: Thomson,
1960–90.
This annual index lists book reviews of secondary sources in the humanities from over 700 scholarly periodicals from 1960–90. It is particularly useful for tracking down scholars' responses to new literary criticism, but it provides no excerpts from the reviews.

*ProQuest 3.0*. Online. Ann Arbor: Bell and Howell Information and Learning, 1999– .
See description above under chapter 3.

# 5. Other Reference Tools

## Biographical Sources

*American National Biography*. 24 vols. New York: Oxford UP, 1998.
This is the most comprehensive and contemporary biographical dictionary of influential Americans in all walks of life. It includes individuals who have died as recently as 1995.

*Biography Index: A Cumulative Index to Biographical Material in Books and Magazines*. New York: Wilson, 1946– .
The printed version, published quarterly, provides access to biographical information appearing in over 1,000 English-language periodicals and books, including collections of biographies. It even directs the reader to citations in many standard biographical reference sources. Wilson offers electronic versions on CD-ROM, *WilsonWeb*, and OCLC's *FirstSearch* covering 1984 to the present.

Brown, Susan Windisch, ed. *Contemporary Novelists*. 6th ed. Detroit: Saint James, 1996.
This volume features sketches of about 700 living English language novelists and short-story writers since about 1940.

*Contemporary Authors: A Biobibliographical Guide to Current Authors and Their Work*: Farmington Hills: Gale, 1962– .
Available both in print and in electronic formats, *Contemporary Authors* offers biographical information on modern authors, "including those who

were active prior to 1960 and whose works continue to influence contemporary literature." Over 100,000 current writers, from a variety of disciplines, are listed.

*Current Biography*. New York: Wilson, 1940– .
Available in print and on CD-ROM, *Current Biography* includes lengthy biographical accounts of hundreds of prominent persons in many occupations and of many nationalities. The print version is published eleven times a year with bound annual cumulations. As of 1986, the cumulations are titled *Current Biography Yearbook*.

*Dictionary of American Biography*. 21 vols. New York: Scribner's, 1928–37. Ten supps., 1944–95.
The *DAB* contains lengthy biographical accounts of prominent deceased Americans. The articles are written and signed by authoritative contributors. There are six general indexes covering all volumes through the eighth supplement: names of the subjects, contributors of the biographies, birthplaces, schools, occupations, and general topics. The ninth supplement has a name index covering all the supplements.

*Dictionary of Literary Biography*. Farmington Hills: Gale Group, 1978– .
This is one of the most comprehensive and useful biographical encyclopedias of literary figures, both living and deceased. It is available in print and on the Internet as part of the *GaleNet* service. Each of the printed volumes is devoted to authors of a particular nationality, writing in a particular genre during a specified literary period. For example, volume 9 is entitled *American Novelists, 1910–1945*. The entries are lengthy, well-illustrated, and critical and are written by appropriate scholars. They include selective bibliographies of primary and secondary sources, which often note the location of manuscripts and archives. In 1981, Gale introduced *The Dictionary of Literary Biography Yearbook*, which updates and expands the coverage of authors discussed in their regular printed series and adds entries for authors previously overlooked. The electronic version permits searching by a variety of methods (author's name, titles, subjects/themes, genre, nationality, etc.) including any keyword in the entry.

*Dictionary of National Biography*. 22 vols. London: Oxford UP, 1967–68.
The *DNB* is the British equivalent of the *DAB*. The lengthy scholarly articles on prominent Britons, including colonial Americans, are signed by their authors. Supplementary volumes update the set through 1990. The *Concise DNB*, published in 1992, covers the most prominent *DNB* subjects through 1985. It is also available on CD-ROM.

*Literary Index*. Farmington Hills: Gale Group, 1999. <http://www .galenet.com/servlet/LitIndex/>.
This is a master index to the Gale literature series, including *Contemporary Authors*, *Dictionary of Literary Biography*, and all the literary criticism series. Users will need to consult the print volumes for the full text.

Mainiero, Lina, ed. *American Women Writers: A Critical Reference Guide from Colonial Times to the Present*. 4 vols. New York: Ungar, 1979–82. Supp., 1994.
This source provides biographical information and critical discussions on American women writers of fiction and nonfiction, "those who are known and read, and those who have been generally neglected or undervalued because they are women." A two-volume abridged edition was published in 1982.

*Notable American Women, 1607–1950*. 3 vols. Cambridge: Harvard UP, 1971. Supp. by *Notable American Women: The Modern Period*. 1980.
Most of the 1,350 biographical accounts in the three main volumes do not duplicate material in the *DAB*.

Riggs, Thomas, ed. *Contemporary Dramatists*. 6th ed. Farmington Hills: St. James, 1999.
This tool offers brief biographical and bibliographical notes on about 350 playwrights. A list of published works appears under each entry. There is a supplementary section on screenwriters, radio writers, television writers, librettists, and theater groups.

———, ed. *Contemporary Poets*. 6th ed. Detroit: St. James, 1996.
This source provides brief biographical and bibliographical information on some 800 poets writings in English. The format resembles *Contemporary Dramatists*.

## In Quest of Quotations

*Bartlett, John. *Familiar Quotations*. 16th ed. Boston: Little, 1992.
This standard collection of quotations has a keyword index that directs the reader to their authors. Selections listed under the same author are arranged chronologically. Various editions of *Familiar Quotations* are also available on CD-ROM from a variety of publishers including Grolier Interactive and Time Warner Electronic Publishing. *Microsoft Bookshelf CD-ROM Reference Library* also includes *Familiar Quotations*. You can

find it on the Web on Columbia University's *Project Bartleby* (http://www .columbia.edu/acis/bartleby/bartlett).

Maggio, Rosalie, comp. *The Beacon Book of Quotations by Women*. Boston: Beacon, 1992.
Since women have not traditionally been well represented in the standard quotation dictionaries, this guide attempts to fill that gap.

*\*The Oxford Dictionary of Quotations*. Rev. 4th ed. New York: Oxford UP, 1996.
This dictionary provides a useful complement to Bartlett's *Familiar Quotations,* especially in its coverage of literature and the works of women writers. It is organized around the source of the quotation and includes a keyword index.

*Spevack, Marvin. *The Harvard Concordance to Shakespeare*. Cambridge: Harvard UP, 1973.
Based on the text of *The Riverside Shakespeare*, this concordance, generated by computer, picks out the keywords in all the plays and poems.

## Facts from Dictionaries and Handbooks

Dictionaries and Thesauri

*Britannica*. Online. Chicago: Encyclopaedia Britannica, 1994–99. <http:// www.eb.com>.
This is the online version of the *Encyclopaedia Britannica*. The online version includes the complete encyclopaedia, *Merriam-Webster's Collegiate Dictionary*, and the *Britannica Book of the Year*. Advanced searching capabilities make this source more flexible and useful than its printed counterpart.

*Microsoft Bookshelf 98 Reference Library*. Redmond: Microsoft, 1998.
*Microsoft Bookshelf,* typical of CD-ROM sources, provides a variety of standard reference works including dictionary, thesaurus, encyclopedia, and so forth.

*\*Oxford English Dictionary*. 2nd ed. 20 vols. Oxford: Clarendon-Oxford UP, 1989.
The *OED* is the major etymological dictionary of the English language. Its purpose is to outline the history of every word recorded since 1150. Each entry includes the date of introductory use as well as the variant definitions, spellings, and pronunciations over the last 800 years, with

examples of printed usage. There are online and CD-ROM versions. A major new edition of the *OED* is currently in production. The online version of the second edition will be updated every three months with new and revised material. This updating is expected to take until 2010. The project will result in a new online and printed edition.

*Random House Dictionary of the English Language.* 2nd ed. New York: Random, 1987.

*\*Webster's Third New International Dictionary of the English Language.* Springfield: Merriam, 1993.

These two unabridged dictionaries present the language as used currently, without qualifications and censorial omissions.

*Roget's II: The New Thesaurus.* 3rd ed. Boston: Houghton, 1995.

This thesaurus is organized alphabetically.


Literary Handbooks


Andrews, William L., Francis Smith Foster, and Trudier Harris. *The Oxford Companion to African American Literature.* New York: Oxford UP, 1997.

This handbook, the first Oxford Companion specifically devoted to African American literature, features biographical profiles, descriptions of important works, literary characters, genres, and customs. The companion often contains biographical information on authors not easily found in other reference books.

Benét, William Rose. *Benét's Reader's Encyclopedia.* 4th ed. New York: Crowell, 1996.

This standard handbook contains brief articles on literary periods, movements, terms, concepts, allusions, plots, characters, and writers. The latest edition emphasizes twentieth-century and non-Western literatures.

Bordman, Gerald, ed. *The Oxford Companion to American Theatre.* 2nd ed. New York: Oxford UP, 1992.

Although this handbook concentrates on American stage productions as opposed to written drama, students of literature can find a considerable amount of information here, especially in the entries for several hundred major American plays.

*Davidson, Cathy N., and Linda Wagner-Martin. *The Oxford Companion to Women's Writings in the United States.* New York: Oxford UP, 1995.

This source has a specific focus on the writings of American women and includes some excellent essays on many topics not easily found in similar reference books.

*Drabble, Margaret, ed. *The Oxford Companion to English Literature*. Rev. 5th ed. New York: Oxford UP, 1998.
This guide provides short summaries of British literary works, definitions of terms, discussions of movements or trends, and brief biographies and bibliographies of writers.

*Hart, James D., ed. *The Oxford Companion to American Literature*. 6th ed. New York: Oxford UP, 1995.
This source provides short summaries of American literary works, definitions of terms, discussions of movements or trends, and brief biographies and bibliographies of writers.

Hartnoll, Phyllis, and Peter Found. *The Concise Oxford Companion to the Theatre*. New York: Oxford UP, 1992.
This new concise edition updates the fourth edition of *The Oxford Companion to the Theatre*, published in 1983. It covers all aspects of world theater, historical and contemporary. The focus is primarily on performances rather than on written texts, but it can prove useful for students of literature.

*New Princeton Encyclopedia of Poetry and Poetics*. Princeton UP, 1993.
"This is a book of knowledge, of facts, theories, questions, and informed judgment, about poetry. Its aim is to provide a comprehensive, comparative, reasonably advanced, yet readable reference for all students, teachers, scholars, poets, or general readers interested in the history of any poetry in any national literatures of the world, or in any aspect of the technique or criticism of poetry" (vii).

## Guidelines on Form

Ballenger, Bruce. *The Curious Researcher: A Guide to Writing Research Papers*. Boston: Allyn and Bacon, 1998.
Although this guide does not specifically deal with literary research, it is a very good guide to basic, undergraduate-level research in a variety of disciplines, including literature.

*EndNote*. CD-ROM. Philadelphia: Inst. for Scientific Information ResearchSoft, 1998.

*ProCite*. CD-ROM. Philadelphia: Inst. for Scientific Information, 1998.

These management software programs produce properly formatted bibliographies of citations retrieved from electronic databases, in accordance
with a variety of standards, including Modern Language Association of
America. They also allow you to store and sort extensive files of bibliographic records at your desktop. This is especially helpful for large research projects. Each has some distinct features. *EndNote* lets you format
full in-text notes and bibliography at the same time. *ProCite* will build a
keyword list automatically from your files. *EndNote* allows you to connect
directly to Internet databases. *ProCite* will accept a downloaded search,
but will not connect directly to the Internet from within the program.
With each upgraded version, new features are added.

*Gibaldi, Joseph. *MLA Handbook for Writers of Research Papers*. 5th ed.
      New York: MLA, 1999
This manual presents a set of "commonly agreed-on rules of documenting
quotations, facts, opinions, and paraphrases" (xiv). There are lots of tips
for writing a good research paper. This edition is especially helpful with
electronic resources and citations.

# 6. Primary Sources

This listing represents only a few of the many primary sources available. They have been selected for their breadth of coverage. There are
many large microform sets covering a variety of topics, such as the
*History of Women* collection, as well as reputable Web sites featuring
primary material, such as the Library of Congress's *American Mem-
ory*. There are also several major sets listing the works published during a particular period in the United Kingdom and in the United
States. Many of the titles listed in these short title catalogs, some of
which are accessible electronically, are available in microform collections. One example is the *English Short Title Catalogue* (or *ESTC*), an
online listing of materials published in Great Britain and the United
States from 1475 through 1800. Several microform sets, such as *The
Eighteenth Century*, have reproduced the items included. Check with
your reference librarian to find out what is available in your library.

*CIS U.S. Congressional Committee Hearings Index, 1833–1969*. Washing-
      ton: Congressional Information Service, 1981–85.
This printed index to congressional hearings covers the period from 1833
to 1969. See the next listing for electronic versions.

*Congressional Masterfile I, Congressional Masterfile II, Congressional Universe.* Washington: Congressional Information Service, various dates.

These sources index the hearings and other publications of the United States congress. *Congressional Masterfile I*, on CD-ROM, covers the period from 1789 to 1969 and *Congressional Masterfile II*, also on CD-ROM, begins with 1970. *Congressional Universe*, available on the Web by subscription, provides coverage since 1970 and includes the full text of hearings and other congressional publications from 1993 to the present.

*Great Britain. Parliament. *Parliamentary Debates, 1803–* . London: pub. varies, 1804– .

Generally cited as *Hansard* or *Hansard's Parliamentary Debates*, this set indexes the debates of the House of Lords and the House of Commons.

*New York Times Index*. New York: pub. varies, 1851– .

This subject index to the *New York Times* covers the period from 1851 to the present.

*Palmer's Index to the *Times *Newspaper, 1790–1941*. London: Palmer, 1868–1943.

A subject index to the *Times* (London), this index is also available on CD-ROM for the years 1790 to 1905 from Chadwyck-Healey. After 1906, an index was published by the *Times* and is available in many large libraries.

*Poole's Index to Periodical Literature, 1802–1881*; supplements, 1882–1906. Boston: Houghton, 1802–1906.

*Poole's* is the major subject index to American and English periodicals published during the nineteenth century. Biographical and critical references to authors are listed under the author's name. This index is now available as a Web subscription under the title *Poole's Plus: The Digital Index of the Nineteenth Century*.

*Reader's Guide to Periodical Literature*. New York: Wilson, 1905– .

The *Reader's Guide* started publication in 1901 with limited coverage and expanded to include additional periodical titles in 1905. All titles are United States publications. Still published today, this index is particularly valuable for the first seventy-five years of the twentieth-century, for which fewer indexing sources are available.

*Wellesley Index to Victorian Periodicals, 1824–1900*. Toronto: U of Toronto, 1966–89.

Organized by periodical title, *Wellesley* indexes 43 nineteenth-century

British periodicals. Under each title, the table of contents for each issue is listed. The index was recently issued in CD-ROM by Routledge, which will greatly enhance its usefulness.

# 7. Pulling It All Together

*Literature Online*. Online. Alexandria: Chadwick-Healey, 1996– .
This database represents the largest collection of literary texts and includes primary sources (poems, plays, and novels) and secondary sources (reference works and literary criticism). *LION* can offer the user one-stop shopping for background on an author, copies of works, and an index to major literary criticism with full text. It also references Gale's *Literary Resource Center*, as appropriate.

*Literary Resource Center*. Online. Farmington Hills: Gale, 1998– .
See entry under chapter 3 for description.

# 8: Guides to Reference Books

*Balay, Robert. ed. *Guide to Reference Books*. 11th ed. Chicago: Amer. Lib. Assn., 1996.
This guide provides the broadest coverage of major scholarly research tools in all disciplines through 1993. Brief annotations accompany most entries. The literature section is subdivided by type of reference source, by language or nationality, and by author. The index interfiles authors, editors, titles, and subject entries.

Bracken, James K. *Reference Works in British and American Literature*. 2nd ed. Englewood: Libraries Unlimited, 1998.
Volume 1 covers reference works, major journals, research centers, and associations in English and American literature. The arrangement is classified, and there are author-title and subject indexes. The annotations are lengthy and often evaluative. Volume 2 covers individual authors.

*Harner, James L. *Literary Research Guide: An Annotated Listing of Reference Sources in English Literary Studies*. 3rd ed. New York: MLA, 1998.
This guide provides an extensive list of important reference books and periodicals on British and American literature and other literatures in English. The annotations are evaluative, offering keen observations on the quality and usefulness of specific reference sources. In Harner's pref-

ace to the 3rd ed., he claims to have "assessed anew each of the works cited in the second edition and evaluated reference works, print and electronic, that appeared *after* April 1992."

Marcuse, Michael J. *A Reference Guide for English Studies*. Berkeley: U of California P, 1990.

Although now over a decade old, this guide remains an excellent annotated bibliography in this field. Marcuse defines English studies as "any critical and scholarly inquiry presently pursued by members of university departments of English language and literature" (ix). These areas include English and American literature, theater, drama, film, literary theory, rhetoric, and composition, among others. This guide provides information that you typically will not find in similar works, such as descriptions of important library collections, lists of national bibliographies, and listings of library catalogs.

# Index

By Lorena O'English